Status
Passage

Status

Passage

Barney G. Glaser
Anselm L. Strauss

ALDINETRANSACTION
A Division of Transaction Publishers
New Brunswick (U.S.A.) and London (U.K.)

First paperback edition 2010

Library of Congress Catalog Number: 2009036901
ISBN: 978-0-202-36338-7
Printed in the United States of America

Library of Congress Cataloging-in-Publication Data

Glaser, Barney G.
    Status passage / Barney G. Glaser and Anselm L. Strauss.
        p. cm.
    Includes bibliographical references and index.
    ISBN 978-0-202-36338-7
        1. Social status. 2. Social status--United States. I. Strauss, Anselm L. II. Title.

HM821.G55 2009
305--dc22

2009036901

CONTENTS

PREFACE

THOSE of our readers who are acquainted with *The Discovery of Grounded Theory* will remember the distinctions made there between substantive and formal theory[1] and our assertion that social scientists develop substantive theory with relative ease compared to their generation of grounded (nonspeculative) formal theory. We remarked on the suspicion toward more general theories entertained by many social scientists, certainly by sociologists — after three decades of Parsons and other "logico-deductive" theorists — and we noted the propensity of many to settle for less general theories. In that earlier book, we outlined a means for generating formal theories through comparative analyses of multiple substantive areas. At the time, we

1. Barney G. Glaser and Anselm L. Strauss, *The Discovery of Grounded Theory,* (Chicago: Aldine Publishing Co., 1967). By *substantive theory* we mean that theory developed for a substantative or empirical area of sociological inquiry, such as patient care, race relations, professional education, delinquency, or financial organizations. By *formal theory* we mean that theory developed for a formal or conceptual area of sociological inquiry, such as stigma, deviant behavior, socialization, status congruency, authority and power, reward systems, or oganizational careers.

had developed no such theories; we only had some notions about how they might be generated through theoretical sampling and their comparative analysis.

Our aims in publishing the present volume are twofold. First, we present the results of an attempt to develop a formal theory about status passages, hoping that however deficient readers may find the product they will be sufficiently stimulated by it to improve our methods. Had we known of similar ventures using the same means, then of course we should not have had the temerity to advertise them as worthy of emulation. Our second more pragmatic aim is to generate formal theory that is potentially useful for studying status passages, wherever they may occur. We chose to theorize about status passages because of a long standing interest in this fascinating social phenomenon and because this universal phenomenon of passage through statuses is so deserving of a formal theory.

While our writing in this book is at a fairly abstract level, we think that even the layman who is willing to follow the development of the theory, point by point, may profit in his understanding of society and possibly even in the management of his own life. We would like to believe that professionals (in fields such as social work, gerontology, nursing, delinquency) as well as social scientists concerned with matters such as socialization, work, leisure, mobility and organizations, might gain something from our theory.

We wish to express thanks, for their useful criticism and suggestions, to three readers of the original manuscript: Rue Bucher and Joanne Stelling of the Department of Psychiatry, College of Medicine, University of Illinois, Chicago Circle; and Norman Denzin of the Department of Sociology, University of California, Berkeley. And as usual, we are grateful to the indispensable Mrs. Elaine McLarin and to Mrs. Shelia Krasow for converting scribbling and messy typing into clear type script and for meeting all those inevitable deadlines that dog most authors.

1. STATUS PASSAGES AND THEIR PROPERTIES

THE PHENOMENA of status passages[1] were enduringly called to the attention of social scientists by Arnold van Gennep's *Les rites de passage*.[2] In that book, the French scholar remarked on various types of passages between what, in modern vocabulary, are termed statuses. Mainly he analyzed such passages as those which occur between age-linked statuses, such as birth and childhood, adolescence and adulthood, and being unmarried and married. Those kinds of passages have, of course, been much studied since van Gennep's day, especially by anthropologists.[3] Sociologists have also expended considerable

1. The first section of this chapter is taken, with slight changes, from a paper by Anselm Strauss, "Some Neglected Properties of Status Passage" in H. S. Becker *et al, Institutions and the Person* (Chicago: Aldine Publishing Company, 1968)

2. Translated by M. Vizedom and G. Cafee (Chicago: University of Chicago Press, 1960). The book was first published in 1908.

3. For some of the anthropological literature, see the bibliography in Max Gluckman (Ed.), *Essays on the Ritual of Social Relations* (Manchester: Manchester University, Press, 1962). The essays by Meyer Fortes, Daryll Forde, and Victor Turner illustrate the kinds of analysis offered by contemporary British anthropologists of "status change" (Fortes' term).

1

effort studying status passages that occur within occupations (careers and socialization, for instance) and within organizations (mobility, for instance). Such passages may entail movement into a different part of a social structure; or a loss or gain of privilege, influence, or power, and a changed identity and sense of self, as well as changed behavior.

One of the hallmarks of status passages, especially ones deemed important by passagees or other interested parties, is the astonishingly frequent and free discussion of passages, for these are open rather than tabooed topics. Their very existence points to vital personal and social concerns — as reflected by van Gennep's initial choice of examined passages — or at least quite absorbing interests. The talk itself is an immensely varied provider of properties of status passage. It may, for example in recruiting, be directed at a potential passagee, to describe or advise him about his future steps. The recruiter may idealize the passage for the passagee to persuade him to embark on the passage if he either seems reluctant to begin the passage or wishes to withdraw after an initial trial in it. The recruiter may also dissuade him from attempting it. The passagee also talks in a variety of modes about his impending passage, and to whom he talks and in what characteristic mode is likely to be socially patterned. Agents in his future passage also talk about him, to each other and to him, in patterned ways.

Passages themselves are continually discussed by participants. They may receive both general support and redefinition, either in part (some of the steps or division of labor among agents should perhaps be changed) or virtually *en toto*. Because status passages frequently are associated with the functioning of organizations and institutions, public debate about passages is very likely to be prominent in any discussion about organizational or institutional change, including that which has already occurred or should occur or expectably will occur.

No wonder, then, that social scientists have been interested in status passages and have found them relatively easy to research, whether they are isolated for special study or examined as segments of a larger social context. Indeed, we would argue on two grounds that status passages deserve a great deal more study. Insofar as every social structure requires manpower, men are recruited by agents to move along through social positions or statuses. Status is a resting place for individuals. But while the status itself may persist for many years, no matter how long an individual remains in, say, an office, there is an implicit or even explicit date when he must leave it. The following statement applies to most: "A temporal dimension is implicit in all kinds of status. No one is assigned, nor may he assume, a position or status forever. Always there is a clause, whether hidden or openly acknowledged, whereby a man may be dispossessed or may dispossess himself of the status."[4] For the potentially profitable purposes of research, the social scientists has only to look at a person and ask, "What passages is he going through today?" or look at an event while asking, "What passage is occurring, and who is playing what roles in it?"

A second reason for believing that status passages deserve more — and more explicit — study is that they reflect conditions for and changes in social structure and its functioning; and these changes may have consequences for the social structure. We particularly emphasize this point because a principal (and limiting) feature of most status passages studied implicitly by anthropologists and sociologists is their relatively scheduled character. These passages are governed by fairly clear rules concerning when the change of status should be made, by whom and by whose agency. There are also prescribed sequences of steps the person must go through to have completed the passage and regularized actions that must be carried out by various relevant participants in order that the passage actually be accomplished. Scheduling, regularization, and prescription are integral to so many status passages that current analyses naturally have included descriptions of the rituals which tend to accompany at least certain phases of those changes of status. Writings, especially when explicitly focused on status passages, have tended to emphasize the relatively permanent rather than the continual occurence of social change.

Without necessarily being influenced by van Gennep but no doubt affected by anthropological research, sociologists have tended to assume in their analyses that status passages are fairly regularized, scheduled, and prescribed. But those three properties of passage can be absent or present only in some degree in some types of status passage. Furthermore, certain other properties may characterize a type of passage.

Those additional properties include the following:

4. Anselm Strauss, *Mirrors and Masks* (San Francisco: The Sociology Press, 1970), first published in 1959.

1. The passage may be considered in some measure *desirable* or undesirable by the person making the passage or by other relevant parties. Going from unmarried to married status generally is thought desirable; becoming a prisoner is generally undesirable.

2. The passage may be *inevitable.* In van Gennep's book, the passage from birth to childhood is inevitable; in our society, the passage into the marital status is not.

3. The passage may be *reversible* to some degree. The age-graded passages that anthropologists study run in only one direction; they are irreversible. But changes of status within organizations can be reversible — a man can not only move "up" into a status but can also be demoted. Sick people may recover totally or partly.

4. A passage may be *repeatable* or nonrepeatable. Parson's analysis of the sick role focuses on reversibility (from normal to sick and back to normal), but this passage can be repeatable. Cleveland was twice elected President of the United States, even after an intervening defeat, whereas Franklin Roosevelt was elected repeatedly.

5. The person who goes through the passage may do so *alone, collectively,* or in *aggregate* with any number of other persons.[5]

6. It follows that when people go through a passage collectively, or in aggregate, they may not be *aware* that they are all going through it together or at least not aware of all aspects of their similar passages. The experience of virtually any cohorts, such as those of a large school class, provides an example.

7. It is worth distinguishing between the above situation and one where, although aware, the person can or cannot *communicate* with the others. Most often, of course, communication is possible, but there are passages where those being "processed" cannot communicate with others who are simultaneously going through an identical change of status (for instance, junior executives in a large corporation who are simultaneously being demoted.)

8. The person making the passage may do so *voluntarily* or have no choice in the matter (or perhaps have degrees of choice either *en toto* or about aspects of the passage). Commitment to prison after trial

5. Stanton Wheeler has recently called attention to this property as potentially important for studying socialization. See his "The Structure of Formally Organized Socialization Setting," in Orville Brim and Stanton Wheeler, *Socialization after Childhood* (New York: Wiley, 1966), especially pp. 61-66.

is involuntary; commitment to a mental institution may be voluntary or involuntary (or partly both).

9. Another property is the degree of *control* which various agents — including the person undergoing the passage — have over various aspects of the passage. For instance, a prisoner may have some degree of control — through his deportment — over how quickly he can leave the prison on parole. A father can forbid or persuade his son not to take the driving exam that, if passed successfully, will make him a licensed driver.

10. The passage may require special *legitimation* by one or more authorized agents. Thus a man may die, but his death is not official until he is pronounced dead by a legitimate agent: a physician.

11. The *clarity* of the signs of passage, for the various parties, may vary from great to negligible clarity. It is clear to an applicant that he has been accepted into college when he receives notice of his acceptance, but Sutherland's thief describes vividly how a con man turns a man into a mark, without the man's immediate recognition. The signs are not always so clear to the person himself, let alone to relevant parties who, like parents, may not recognize when their children are married.

12. These last examples suggest that the signs might actually be clear enough if they were known, but that they may be *disguised* by relevant parties. (This, of course, is an aspect of control, just as it is of deliberately managed lack of clarity.)

We can assume that this is an incomplete list of the properties of status passage, but it is important to distinguish among them and among their various possible combinations. After reading this list of properties, a colleague immediately suggested, from his own research, two others of obvious importance: (1) The *centrality* of the passage to the person, that is, how much difference it makes to him. This is a property of desirability of a passage. (2) The *length of time or duration* in passage, that is, if it will be very short or very long or somewhere between. This is a temporal property of a passage, which is often scheduled.

As will be argued below, the more explicitly in focus such properties are kept during analyses of status passage, the more *systematic* will be the analyses; further, the more systematic, the better an analyst can account for the behaviors of, and consequences for, the persons involved in any given status passage.

We might add for the benefit of those readers who grow restive when faced with undefined or ill-defined concepts, that we prefer not to define *status passages* but to let the full range of meanings for the concept emerge in this book through the combined references of the data analyzed and the analyses themselves. The list of properties should already suggest that the anthropologists have focused attention on far too limited a range of what could be relatable phenomena.

Problems Of Substantive Analysis

When analyzing status passages, analysts most commonly and naturally highlight those properties which seem particularly relevant. Julius Roth has focused on the indeterminate pace of recovery from severe tuberculosis, the ambiguity of the signs of recovery especially as the patient sees the signs, and the patient's manipulations with respect to getting his condition defined "upward" by the legitimating physician.[6] Similarly, when writing of polio patients and their families,[7] Fred Davis dwelt mainly on recovery and its ambiguous signs as, when writing of degradation ceremonies, Harold Garfinkel almost inevitably focused on legitimacy and control: the degrading agent must manage to legitimate his activity and his role to make his accusation persuasive.[8] Orrin Klapp's analysis of how people are made into fools also had its appropriate focus: the successful or unsuccessful strategies of the foolmaker, and of the person who either manages or fails to avoid that status and who manages or fails to reverse the passage once cast into the status.[9] Howard Becker and his associates placed primary emphasis on the collective passage of medical students through medical school and their close communication on matters related to control of passage.[10] One last example: Lloyd Warner's

6. Julius Roth, *Timetables* (Indianapolis: Bobbs-Merrill, 1963).

7. Fred Davis, *Passage through Crisis.* (Indianapolis: Bobbs-Merrill, 1963).

8. Harold Garfinkel, "Conditions of Successful Degradation Ceremonies," *American Journal of Sociology* (1956), 61: 420-24.

9. Orrin Klapp, "The Fool as a Social Type," *American Journal of Sociology* (1949) 55: 159-60.

10. Howard Becker et al, *Boys in White* (Chicago: University of Chicago Press, 1961).

detailed description of age-grading in an Australian tribe almost necessarily turned around an analysis of sequential and collective passages of status, carefully regulated so that entire segments of the tribe were involved at particular times and places.[11]

Because there are several properties of status passage, these and other existing analyses of given status passages may easily be, and usually are, incomplete when focused exclusively and only on one, two, or three relevant properties of the passage. The author may focus so steadily on a single property or two that he sees no others and no exceptions; or, as with Erving Goffman's idealized (if negatively toned) depiction of the mental patient's moral career, readers may mistake his systematic analysis for the total truth.[12]

If an analyst goes on to only mention additional minor properties of the status passage, rather than analyzing their import and relating them to the core properties and thereby densifying the theory, his analysis is still incomplete. Sometimes such incomplete analysis can be spotted easily because he uses a phrase such as "in general" to qualify his main analysis; for instance, he may assert that "in general such and such is true," but readily admit there are exceptions — he may even explain briefly why there are exceptions — but he does not really offer a full analysis of the conditions causing exceptions, let alone integrate it with his main analysis. Phrases such as "of course" are also used to indicate qualification to the central point. Exceptional groups or personal attributions also may be singled out as not falling under the general proposition, and only brief explanation may be offered to show what happens under those special conditions.

A closely related type of incompleteness is when the analyst actually fails to recognize the relevance of another property that, if properly analyzed, would be of considerable significance and then necessarily woven back into the theory. He recognizes, for instance, that the status passage is voluntary, but the reader has to determine for himself the significance of this property if he thinks to question its significance. In essence, these incomplete analyses brush aside the need for analysis, handle analysis in perfunctory fashion, or do inade-

11. Lloyd Warner, *A Black Civilization* (New York: Harper, 1937).

12. Erving Goffman, "The Moral Career of the Mental Patient" in *Asylums* (Chicago: Aldine Publishing Company, 1961), pp. 125-171.

quate justice to it for lack of sensitivity to other relevant properties of status passage that might be operating.

When the analyst focuses on only one or two properties, the result is a less dense analysis than could be made. True, the researcher may make a very full analysis of each property (for instance, its consequences for interaction, and for various actors, and even for some relevant institution). He may even make a rather integrated analysis combining, let us say, his analysis of two properties. Nevertheless, some perceptive readers will feel, and quite correctly, that the total analysis lacks a certain richness — that it is, as we once heard a first-rate monograph characterized, "disappointingly thin although carefully done." One reason that ethnographers' accounts often appear so rich is precisely because they manage explicitly to weave analysis around the more standard properties, that are conventionally agreed on as worth studying. Of course, they also tend to brush by exceptions quickly or barely to make the kinds of qualifications that sociologists, perhaps, are likely to make because of the less homogeneous populations that they study.[13]

Our contention is that unless a researcher is explicitly sensitive to multiple properties of status passage, he can be expected to make a relatively incomplete analysis of his data. Of course, if he does not recognize that his data can be conceived of as pertaining to status passages, then his analysis must necessarily be incomplete when viewed in that context, though it may certainly be quite stimulating when taken on its own terms.

We shall illustrate by outlining what can be more fully seen about a rather "dense" analysis in one of our books.[14] If we conceive of dying as a passage between statuses, then its major properties appear to be: dying is almost always unscheduled; the sequence of steps is not institutionally prescribed; and the actions of the various participants are only partly regulated. Quite relevant also is that dying (though not necessarily death itself when it comes) is usually defined as undesira-

13. On this same general point see the "post structural" criticism in A. L. Epstein (Ed.) *The Craft of Social Anthropology* (London: Tavistock Publications, 1967), especially the remarks by Max Gluckman in the introduction to the volume, and the papers by J. Van Velsen (pp. 129-149), V. W. Turner (pp. 181-204), and M. G. Marwick (pp. 231-44).

14. Barney G. Glaser and Anselm L. Strauss, *Time for Dying* (Chicago: Aldine Publishing Company, 1968).

ble and is usually involuntary. Among the other relevant but highly variable properties are: the degree to which the signs are disguised; the clarity of signs which are available to the various participants; the amount of control which the participants, including the patient, have over aspects of his passage; the potential reversibility, arrestability, or repeatability of his passage; whether the passage is traversed simultaneously by multiple patients or he alone is dying; and if simultaneously which, if any, patients are aware of particular aspects of the process. Complex permutations of those interrelated properties give rise to the variable social events which occur to and around dying patients. Those events require analysis in relation to interrelated properties. Events should not simply be added, with such provisos as "in general, but," and then related to a property of which the reader never hears again. There should not be numerous tag-ends signaled by implicit qualifying phrases such as "sometimes" and "some patients," and "other patients," without adequate explanations for why "some" or "sometimes."

In short, we suggest that anyone who wishes to develop a substantive analysis about any phenomenon that might also be fruitfully conceived of as a status passage can considerably tighten up, as well as make more "dense," his systematic formulation by guiding his research with a sensitivity to the kinds of properties listed above.[15] Indeed unless he does so, he will fail to note many important behaviors of, and consequences for, the persons involved in the status passage. Very likely, the omissions due to incomplete analysis will skew his conclusions and yield a less systematic formulation. Thus, analysis of voluntary commitment to hospitals would expand the range of Goffman's conclusions about the moral careers of mental patients, and analysis of the potential repeatability of tuberculosis

15. Apropos of this point, but by way of suggestion rather than assertion: in a fine paper on "Ritual and Office in Tribal Society," Fortes, *op. cit.*, has addressed himself to a question raised although not adequately answered by van Gennep: Why "is ritual apparently indispensable in marking status change," (p. 55). Fortes gives a general answer whose accuracy need not concern us here. Our suggestion is that if one thinks in terms of specific properties of status passage, he should find it possible to specify why certain rituals and ceremonies take the form they do. For instance, in terms of control and of desirability, "cooling out" of a failure requires certain types of ritual as compared with rituals that accompany his achieving a desirable status. Also, Norman Denzin has suggested to us the additional points: who employs the rituals and under what conditions — and of course their consequences.

would affect Roth's conclusions about the behavior of the hospitalized tuberculosis patient.

The principle of relevance is still valid, of course: primary analysis should be organized around those core properties which seem especially relevant to the substantive area under study. The analysis of other properties, however, should be made and integrated with the primary analysis. Every paper about status passage need not, of course, include a complete analysis. If an investigator's research is to have richness and integration, however, several properties must be analyzed and integrated during the course of the total investigation.

These suggestions do not negate the importance of researchers' hunches and insights into the genuine relevances in their data.[16] To keep the record straight, we note that the research on dying patients began with two general ideas. One was that dying "took time," was a process. The other idea, derived from painful personal experiences, was that a collusive game of "evasion of the truth" often occurred around dying people. The first idea evolved into a theory of dying trajectories long before we sensed their relevance to status passages; the second evolved organically into a theory of "awareness contexts." Like any formal theory, a theory of status passages should be used with sense and sensitivity and should not close the door on alternatively promising analyses. If we choose, however, to study status passages and to analyze them, we might just as well take a closer and more sustained look at their several properties. Is it not also evident that some reported research would also gain in theoretical relevance and clarity, if the researcher realized that the area he is studying (for instance, parole or commitment studies) might be viewed in status passage terms?[17] Is there any question that such substantive analyses would profit from the prior existence of a higher-order, or formal, theory?

16. Barney G. Glaser and Anselm L. Strauss, "Insight and Theory Development" in *Discovery of Grounded Theory* (Chicago: Aldine Publishing Company, 1967) pp. 251-59.

17. For a recent example of what we mean, see the interesting descriptive account by Dorothy Miller and Michael Schwartz, "County Lunacy Commission Hearings: Some Observations of Commitments to a State Mental Hospital," *Social Problems* (1966). 14: 26-35.

Generating Grounded Formal Theory

When generating a grounded formal theory, *comparative analysis* of data drawn from diverse substantive areas is the most satisfactory method especially, we believe, when coupled with the kinds of *theoretical sampling* described in *The Discovery of Grounded Theory*. The interested reader can find a more complete discussion of theoretical sampling in that book. In chapter 9 we shall outline the method used and our experiences in using it when generating our theory of status passages.

In generating a theory of status passages through such comparative analysis, we have used anecdotal comparisons, as well as actual field data and the published and unpublished research of social scientists. Such materials appear as examples on our pages in about the proportion of the above-water segments of icebergs. These examples function as indicators of that analysis. They should also have other functions for the reader: to be illuminating or clarifying illustrations and to afford temporary relief from the effort of concentrating too long on highly abstract sentences. They should occasionally stimulate him, though less than the propositions themselves, to think about comparable phenomena in his own research data.

Quite as important, however, is that some of these materials are — or should — act as evidence for suggested propositions and hypotheses, the latter two appearing ordinarily on the same page just above the "evidence." Some of this evidence is drawn from sociological studies, some from realms of experience probably shared by our readers. An example of the latter type of data would be a tactic used under specified conditions by an agent (a physician) with a passagee (a patient). Evidential data will be found on virtually every page of the book. Although every reader will not agree that every bit of data is "warranted evidence" (to use Dewey's felicitous term), we do hope readers will not suppose that only materials drawn from actual sociological studies are fully evidential. In our desire to emphasize that the technical literature is full of useful data for generating formal theory, most of the footnotes in this book are designed to suggest that a multitude of interesting materials on status passage can be found in given published researches.

The Organization of this Book

Rather than present the formal theory through a serial consideration of the major properties of status passage, we have elected to organize its formulation around six principal considerations: reversibility, temporality, shape, desirability, circumstantiality, and multiplicity. *Reversibility* includes considerations such as direction, repeatability, arrestability, inevitability, and preventability. *Temporality* has to do with matters such as schedule, regularity, prescribed steps, speed and pace. *Shape* concerns periods, plateaus, and the like, along with the crucial issue of "control" over the passage. In the *desirability* chapter we touch on centrality to the actors, desirability or undesirability of the passage, and its voluntary or involuntary character. *Circumstantiality* implies such matters as whether the passage is made by one person alone or in aggregate or collectively. In another chapter we take up the question of *multiple status passages:* every person is simultaneously engaged in many such passages. The final two chapters consist of an illustrative case study and a discussion of formal theory itself. The former consists of the application of our theory to the temporal aspects of social mobility. Discussion in the latter chapter is based largely on the experiences of writing this book, on teaching formal theory to students, and on giving consultation to colleagues engaged in their own research.

In each chapter (except the last) the main variable is indicated by the chapter title, but all the properties noted earlier will be found cross-cutting each main variable. Each chapter begins with the presentation of major issues raised by consideration of the main dimension discussed in that particular chapter. Each touches on a wide range of conditions, tactics, strategies, actors, interactions, and consequences.

While there is only one central variable to a chapter, our analysis will bring out with specificity how each variable is cross-cut by a number of other variables.[18] In writing up this analysis, necessarily we

18. This kind of analysis is different than a conceptual cross-cutting by definitional construction of a theoretical scheme as, say, in Parsons' writing.

have had to emphasize certain cross-cuts, and to subordinate or omit others. The principle behind our selection always was relevance in terms of our own research experience and interests. Readers will wish to add to the analysis — and we urge them to do so — by making further cross-cuts among variables that have been slighted or ignored in this book; in this way, the theory can be progressively extended and made more powerful. Those purposes can be accomplished either by formal analysis such as ours or by analyzing data on particular substantive areas, whether old data now reconsidered or new data collected specifically with status passage theory in mind.

If readers will attempt these types of analyses, they will thereby be testing the usefulness and checking the validity of the theory offered in this small volume. We have deliberately presented the theory in processual and "dense" form rather than as arrays or sets of propositions, because we believe it can better be employed as a working tool whereby colleagues will extend, modify and qualify it.[19] See discussion of this type of theory presentation in *Discovery of Grounded Theory.*[20]

While the density of discussion would help readers who do not mind studying the discussion closely, its very density and abstract quality are likely to cause slower reading than most of us are accustomed to. Hence, throughout the book, a policy of italicizing key concepts and phrases (especially those concerned with "conditions") is followed. This does not mean, however, that non-italicized sentences are not of theoretical importance; they only refer to other types of statements, such as tactics and consequences.

19. And "to negate" it, as others might say; although we would say that only specific hypotheses get negated but theory gets modified, qualified, and extended. For further discussion of this point, see Chapter 9.
20. Pages 31-32. See also our discussion in Chapter 9 of this book.

2. REVERSIBILITY

BECAUSE a status passage is constantly in motion, a major concern of the passagee and agents involved in it is whether the passage is either reversible or nonreversible. In this chapter we shall discuss many facets of reversibility and nonreversibility.

Nonreversibility

Two conditions lead to nonreversibility. The direction of the passage may be *inevitable,* no matter what efforts might be made to stop it by the passagee or agents. Aging is an example of an inevitable passage, as even the heroine of *Lost Horizons* discovered. Reverses in the passage are *preventable;* that is, the passagee or agents have the power to ensure that no changes occur in the direction of the passage. Being drafted is logically reversible. However, because reverses are usually preventable by the draft board, most draftees on receiving their induction notice consider the draft nonreversible. To be sure, some may try to discover ways out when they view such a passage as highly undesirable. Organizations have recently developed to help a potential draftee prevent the passage. This condition may reduce in some measure the inevitability of the passage.

INEVITABLE PASSAGE

Chronic disease, dying and the life cycle (aging) are the inevitable passages that easily come to mind. It is difficult to think of others which cannot be reversed or blocked somehow, by someone, no matter how inevitable they appear. The inevitability of these particular passages requires that there be institutions and organizations to manage, direct, and control them. The principal institutions are education, family, welfare and medicine with the corresponding organizations: schools, homes, social services, hospitals and clinics. These organizations are set up to direct the passages during many, but not all, phases.

To the degree that the phasing and rate of passage is clearly *determinate* (as age-graded education is in the United States) organizations (the primary school) can be delineated for handling specific transitional statuses within the total passage. When the transitional phasing and rate of passage is not determinate, organizations are, then, prepared to manage the passagee's direction for as long as it takes to move him to the next transitional status. Thus, a hospital is prepared to remain in custody over a dying passagee until it is time to send the terminal patient home, to another hospital, to a nursing home, or to a funeral parlor. The less determinate the inevitable passage, the more flexible must the organization be in managing its movement. Hospitals must wait to see how an acute illness passage is progressing. Schools graduate and drop students on schedule; holding people back is infrequent. The mobilization of resources and responsibility and shifts in relationships perforce are also more flexible in organizations designed to manage the less determinant passage.

One property of these indeterminant, inevitable passages is the emergence of *false reversals:* the direction of the passage seems to stop or virtually to reverse itself, but actually it does not. The organization must be prepared to handle these "reversals" on a surprise basis, as when there is a temporary reversal in cases of terminal cancer or serious multiple sclerosis. Such false reversals may even be typical of non-reversible passages, however unscheduled their timing. The organizational personnel or organizations must be prepared to handle the knotty social and psychological problems of passagees and their families and friends when the desirable, but false, reversal leads to unrealistic hopes.

Sometimes a *false but undesirable reversal* (from an organizational standpoint) will occur in a determinate passage that is being managed and controlled on a routine basis, with no great preparation to be flexible. Thus, chaos in the organization's work and sentimental order may result,[1] but only when the reversal is relevant to the routine of the organization. Elderly movie stars who publicly make themselves look younger for vanity's sake and their public images may jeopardize their roles and the success of movies themselves when they are supposed to play their actual age. But when a senior citizen in a nursing home decides to become a "Lady Clairol" blonde, the organization of the home probably will not be affected; the move may even cause some amusement, which helps the personnel's morale.

Although genuinely inevitable, both passagee and his agents may not accept this fact and still try "everything" to halt an undesirable passage. In our studies of dying, we have discussed many strategies which patients, families, and staffs use to cope with the inevitability of dying.[2] Often agents will not disclose to the passagee the direction of the passage, or even its existence, in order to forestall potential psychological consequences such as "giving up," suicide, or deep depression. Even if told, the passagee might deny the inevitability of his passage. Physicians may enlist his cooperation to work hard at stopping the inevitable by using experimental research drugs. Usually, however, their effort is directed only at slowing down the passage as much as possible, even to the point of prolonging the patient's life for some time. Often physicians and nurses work hard just to be "doing something" so as not to give up a life without fighting.

In handling dying, the staff may attempt to reduce an intense realization of the inevitable by getting the patient through painful crises with drugs or even by putting him into a permanent drugged coma during his last days. The staff may also give his kinsmen sedatives to help them cope with the end of the inevitable passage. The life

1. Barney G. Glaser and Anselm L. Strauss, *Time For Dying* (Chicago: Aldine Publishing Company, 1968).

2. *A Case Study of a Dying Trajectory, Ibid.; Awareness of Dying* (Chicago: Aldine Publishing Company, 1965); and *Anguish* (San Francisco: The Sociology Press, 1970).

cycle and many chronic diseases end in death. The degree to which such an end is undesirable, hence something to avoid, will vary inversely with the desirability of the last stages of the passage. People whose dying or chronic disease is, both physically and emotionally, terribly painful to all concerned may crave their own deaths as may the bystanders.

When an inevitable passage is intensely undesirable for all concerned, those people close to the passagee may feel the need to be released from involvement. This amounts to a mutual status passage, where one person is dragging the other through great discomfort. The releasibility of these other people varies considerably. Wives can get divorced or run off. Friends and relatives disappear, fade away, or simply become inattentive — as happens with people who have worsening neurological symptoms. The "out" mechanisms of medical and nursing staff are legion, but are likely to be linked, whether by personal or organizational design, to replacement by another staff member who can stand being responsible for the passage — at least for a time. In any event, the inevitable, undesirable passage may render very unstable all relationships, even the most cherished.

PREVENTABLE REVERSIBILITY

Reversibility that is preventable is of strategic sociological significance. The *nonreversible passage might be reversed, but the agents in control or passagees do not act to reverse it.* They fail to act either because they do not actually perceive that they can, or they do not wish to. An example of the latter is the situation in which physicians have died from the very diseases in which they are specialists by failing to care for themselves. When especially undesirable passages — such as being drafted, sent to the electric chair, or fired — occur, masses of people may rise in protest against the powers who enforce the non-reversibility of the passage.

Another facet of prevented nonreversibility occurs when people put forth great effort to ensure that an easily reversible, but desirable passage becomes nonreversible. The typical example is an occupational career in which the passagee and his friends and sponsors try to bring the unstable, tentative career to where it is virtually nonreversible. The academic tries to reach tenure; the military officer tries to rise high enough in the ranks to be invulnerable to the efforts of colleagues who might prevent him from rising higher; the corporate executive tries to build an informal colleagual system of support and so put himself at a level of the corporate hierarchy that insures his climb to the top. In all these instances, the effort is to gain the power which ensures non-reversibility of passage.

Education is a prominent social mechanism for making a desirable passage nonreversible. The basic assumption is that education and its accoutrements "stick." Thus, when a passagee becomes parted from the agents who have trained him, the passagee himself will have enough self-sufficiency to keep going in the right direction. He will not revert to his older ways in, say, work or social position. Thus, professional and theological schools indoctrinate. Healers give therapy. Schools give degrees to open doors with certification and to help shore up the nonreversibility of a job and career. States give licenses to practice. The agents who have responsibility for training, indoctrinating, or healing try not to release the passagee until reasonably sure that the education will stick. Some indoctrinations take several years. Scheduled training passages require the passagee leave, irrespective of potential reversals. Sometimes agents will never completely let their passagees go. They may thereby prevent the actual reversibility of a passage that would occur when the indoctrination or theory proves too weak to withstand adverse forces. Social workers and public health nurses keep tabs on poor people who have terminated therapy, whether physical or psychological therapy. Alcoholics Anonymous and Synanon provide this support to addicts, much as physicians and ministers do. Sponsors keep track of their protégés.

Agents involved in turning out a passagee, who hopefully will be able to make his own passage nonreversible, are mindful of the relevant social forces that continually — unless blocked — can undermine the direction of a passage. A major example is, of course, the existence of former personal relationships that pull the person back to old ways (*e.g.* convicts on parole). Another is engaging in generally approved relationships that for a particular passage would cause reversal (marriage for the Catholic priest). Yet another is recidivism that occurs from lack of practice because conditions bar or inhibit the passage. Quite difficult to overcome is the distrust or recalcitrance of the passagee in a training or therapy program, for he may accuse the agent of pursuing purely self-interested goals. Until and unless his attitude changes, the agent cannot withdraw without expecting a reversal in passage. Thus, agents over desirable passages, which, however, may seem undesirable to the passagee, may start or administer custodial or supervisory institutions. Typical institutions are "homes," clinics, and prisons. The passagee is kept or sent there for that length of time that agents (judicial or otherwise) believe is necessary to ensure non-reversibility after the passagee is freed. In their judgment, if reversibility without their control is a likely outcome, the passagee is kept permanently in custody. If the prospect of nonreversibility occurs faster than expected, however, the passagee may be watched by planned contracts, such as being on parole or out-patient basis.

Agents in control of an undesirable passage, which they attempt to make nonreversible, may easily have a difficult time in recruiting passagees. Then they might engage in a process of *hooking*. First, they tempt the prospective passagee with bait that by design almost cannot be refused. For example, a con man offers unexpected large profits, and a pusher offers a cost-free trip on a drug. This makes the passage seem desirable for the moment at least. A passagee who then becomes involved is coached along slowly to where he cannot give up the passage even when it becomes undesirable, because of loss of pleasure or fear of pain from physical and social reprisal sources. He becomes addicted, totally absorbed to the exclusion of all else.[3] He is hooked and the passage is virtually nonreversible. Personally or socially he is locked in by conditions. Making a break appears impossible.

The management of awareness contexts[4] *is, of course, crucial in the hooking process.* The passagee is kept from all information that may interfere with or negate the desirability of the bait by confirming the passage's true undesirability. A primary fact kept from him may be that the controlling agent is acting illegitimately or with negative intentions. Also kept from view are clear indicators of the passage's

3. See Marvin B. Scott, *The Racing Game*, (Chicago: Aldine Publishing Company, 1968), Chapter 5; and Ned Polsky, *Hustlers, Beats and Others* (Chicago, Aldine Publishing Company, 1967), chapter on The Hustler; Alfred Lindesmith, *Addiction and Opiates* (Chicago: Aldine Publishing Company).

4. By *awareness context* we refer to who knows what about the issue at stake, which is a contextual condition which people in the situation take into account in words and actions. See Glaser and Strauss, *Awareness,* and Barney G. Glaser and Anselm L. Strauss, "Awareness Contexts and Social Interaction," *American Sociological Review,* Vol. 29, No. 5, Oct. 1964.

eventual undesirability, such as the potential state of deterioration from drug use. The agent attempts at the same time to create a favorable, open (but false) awareness to entice the prospect into passage. (Should negating information break through the closed awareness context, suspicion or its confirmation occurs and the passagee may reverse his passage before it becomes nonreversible.)

Hooking processes may also be used to entice a passagee into what seems to some degree an undesirable passage but which agents know will later prove very desirable to him. Children sometimes have to be baited initially with immediate and pleasurable rewards to go to school or to begin taking music lessons. Stock brokers sometimes have to give a wary, recalcitrant, but potential, investor quick profits as an incentive to get him involved in what looks to him like a dangerous business — the stock market — where soon he can pursue a sensible, conservative career as an investor. Getting people started over the undesirable hump, so to speak, is considered legitimate by the agent. It requires deft management of awareness contexts during the initial phases. For instance, while a draftee is being "desocialized" in a reception center and is cursing the undesirable passage that lies ahead, officially he is told of the many civilian careers for which a soldier may train in army schools.[5] The rigors of basic training are carefully not mentioned. The question of whether the passagee indeed will find the passage really desirable is resolved by the passagee's particular experience.[6]

Another basic societal strategy that control agents use in getting passagees into undesirable, non-reversible passages is through some form of dragnet. This mechanism of recruitment corresponds territorially with the jurisdiction of the control agent. Police "work" cities; sheriffs "work" counties; health officials may "work" the city, county, or the entire state when picking up the mentally ill or contagious TB cases. The FBI "works" the nation. Banks set up dragnets

5. Robert K. Merton and Alice K. Rossi, "Contributions to the Theory of Reference Group Behavior," in *Social Theory and Social Structure* (New York: The Free Press, 1957), revised.

6. People who hesitate over the relative desirability of two different passages can also be hooked by canny agents for one passage. Medical residents who hesitate between practice and academic careers may be hooked by agential tactics such as getting them research money or excellent academic jobs. This example is taken from Rue Bucher's project on "Socialization."

through local agencies to catch people who skip out on loans to other states. When found, the agents do not have to, though they may, hook these passagees. They are usually caught and put in custody, and their feelings on desirability are not pertinent to agents.

Whether hooked or caught in an undesirable passage, perhaps the only out for a passagee when reverses are prevented, is a complete breakout or escape. Usually this is attempted with poor odds for success for prevented nonreversible passages. Prevention techniques cover escapes as one form of reversibility. Once free, the chances of being hooked or caught again depend on where the successful person escapes to and how well he can resist his previous indoctrination into the passage, an indoctrination which presses him to return to the passage. (Delinquency, drug addiction, etc.). Destroying the passage while within it is virtually impossible for single passagees, and infrequent for a mass of them, because destruction comes only with disappearance of the control agents, and the ideas they implement when creating and managing the passage. Whether desirable or not, change in these areas is slow (for example, changes in hospital or prison systems). Quick changes mean virtual institutional revolution.

Reversibility

Reversibility in a status passage comes from two general sometimes interrelated sources. Structural conditions (both contextual and situational) can render a passage reversible (a company going out of business or having major cuts in budget may reverse the careers of employees). Personal conditions can reverse a passage also, as when either agents, passagees, or both take the steps necessary for some form of reversal, which is feasible and manageable because neither have sufficient power over the others to keep the passage nonreversible. (For example, either a piano student or his teacher may simply quit.)

STRUCTURAL SOURCES OF REVERSIBILITY

Several general, interrelated structural conditions can reverse passages. In some passages, if the passage does not move forward continuously it may be vulnerable to conditions which reverse it. College students who quit school but still intend to study are subject to reversals when marital and occupational conditions flood their lives and prevent their continuing to study on their own. Another example is the "up or out" rule for promotions that affects careers in many organizations, as it does in universities. In the rehabilitation and treatment passages that are provided for addicts, criminals, and the mentally ill, the probability of reversals is often high. Such passages depend on constant movement forward to balance off the pull backward. Without this balance, recidivism would probably occur.

Another structural condition is the emergence of a new passage that necessarily takes priority over current central passages and brings them to a total halt or reversal, at least for the time being. Induction into the armed services may halt an occupational career and sometimes allay, halt, or reverse a passage into or through marriage. An unsuspected illness when discovered can easily cause a reversal in occupational and marital passages. Because of greater priority the new passage becomes central and causes a halt or reversal in other central passages. Without necessary priority, the new passage would not erode a passagee's involvement in other central passages. With less priority it would perhaps only reverse a less important passage, on the order of its own priority within the multiple passages of a person. For example, a new hobby will usually only displace or lessen interest in an older hobby, and conditions which facilitate sail-planing usually lessen the number of persons who devote weekends to flying small planes in the same region.

Another condition, mentioned earlier, is the passage's discontinuance by the structure within which it is embedded. When the organization shuts down, the passagees may, of course, go elsewhere to continue with the identical passage. An editor can seek the same job with another newspaper. Sometimes the discontinuance of the passage is total, or virtually so for a geographical area, because of strikes or technological change. A new method for coal mining can change the occupation forever.[7] A switch in government support can impoverish a university research program. The unemployed must give up his occupation for a new occupation or move to a new region. When a central passage — say, of family or occupation — gets wiped out, the reversal may easily spread to others of the passagee's multiple

7. Fred Cottrell, "Of Time and the Railroader," *American Sociology Review,* April 1939, pp. 190-98.

passages if these depend on the resources from the destroyed passages (loss of funds to support a home, a social life, an important hobby).

Changing structural conditions can also result in a change of direction of a passage, which to the passagee may amount to a reversal. For example, an organization may make a rule that its employees may not accept compensation for consulting with other organizations or may drastically limit the amount of consulting fees; such actions stop a career in consulting. Again, many types of skills have periods of greater and lesser favor in their uses. The computer industry has created a great need for mathematicians and thereby has changed the direction of their possible careers. Some mathematicians may see this as a reversal from academic careers, but others see a chance to get ahead financially. As computers take over work, many clerks, for example, who have kept track of the administrative and organizational accounts, have suffered reversals in their careers. They are phased out as soon as possible, but in the meantime find themselves in blind alley jobs.[8]

A structural condition may generate a crucial incident which occasions a reversal of status passage. For example, something may happen to an agent that prevents his guiding and helping the passagee so that he is in for a reversal until either the agent returns or a new one is found. This occurs in business organizations when a sponsor becomes ill, is transferred, falls into disfavor and is demoted; then his protege may suffer an earlier reversal. Similarly, when a faculty member moves to another University, a graduate student who has been working in his area of research may lose a year or more while moving to another sponsoring faculty man and another research area.[9] In short, a crucial incident, which is allowed to persist, then becomes a structural condition that does not merely block but actually reverses a passage.

The crucial incident is usually an unforeseen accident or disaster. An automobile crash can easily reverse several passages of a person, until or unless he gets well. A narcotic addict who has kicked his habit may realistically fear that physical pain will force him to take a

8. Bernard Levenson, "Bureaucratic Succession," in Amitai Etzioni (Ed.), *Complex Organizations* (New York: Holt, Rinehart and Winston, 1961), pp. 362-76.
9. Personal communication from Rue Bucher regarding biochemistry students studied during a project on "socialization."

narcotic as a painkiller, and so he will be hooked all over again.[10] The degree of probability of such accidents usually is an open question, but if they can be somewhat codified insurance can be sold to help prevent or mitigate at least the financial reversals and their drastic consequences. Of course, some unforeseen conditions cannot be insured against so directly — for instance the subtle blockage of a superordinate's career which in a chain reaction blocks the career of a subordinate.[11] If the subordinate had calculated the probabilities of the unfortunate crucial event, however, he might have evolved options which now leave his career unimpeded ("It pays to hedge your bets.")

Sometimes a condition has been developing for a long time, but neither passagee nor agent has been aware of this, so when it manifests itself it is seen as a crucial incident. Economic breakdown is a typical condition. When the real estate depression of 1965-66 began to appear, many people were not sensitive to information that should have alerted them to the development of a "tight money" condition. When that condition was felt — as when suddenly they were refused loans to carry on businesses associated with building and sales — passages dependent on money were reversed, at least for a time, if not to the point of complete failure. Up to the difficult point most people, who were then caught in the financial reversal, had neither the ability nor the suspicion to attempt gaining information pertaining to the relevant economic conditions. The stock market crash of 1929 was only a more dramatic instance of the same phenomenon.

These general — and interrelated — conditions (keeping the passage moving, new passages having priority, discontinuance of passages, changing structural conditions, crucial incident) set contingency limits to potential reversals. The limits are a matter of degree, fostered by the condition that under examination becomes quite complex.

One aspect, distance, pertains to how far back the reversal may go before either complete failure or re-reversibility must occur. Thus a man can only be demoted so far before demoralization may set in. The particular structural condition (say, an illness) may have built the repeatability both for reversals and re-reversals (comebacks) into the degree of reversal. Built into the degree of reversibility also is the

10. Lindesmith, *op. cit.*
11. Levenson, *op. cit.*

amount of time that elapses. For example, a teacher can punish a pupil for only so long before classmates become angry or even demoralized and, then, not to reverse causes havoc in the classroom. Again, how long can a political candidate suffer the reversal of a poor image before it either must be rectified or he is out of the race?[12]

Another contingency is the probability of the occurrence and severity of reversals. While for some passages calculations of probability about reversals may be impossible or difficult, for others they are possible and predictable. The probability that success in running a small business will be reversed by adverse economic condition can be high, and a severe reversal may easily bring complete failure. By contrast, a reversal in the career of a civil servant is of low probability, and when it occurs is usually of minor severity. If a department is eliminated, for example, a substitute job is easily found and with relatively few attendant problems of transition.

Again, the probable degree and severity of reversal can be ascertained in accordance with what alternative options are provided by the given condition causing the reversal. Some provide few or none. Induction into the service provides few alternatives such as delaying schemes, leaving the country, or becoming a conscientious objector (too drastic an option for most inductees). A violinist who suffers irreparable damage to one hand can no longer play that instrument, though he might teach others to play. When the artist, Henri Matisse, became so arthritic that he could no longer paint effectively, he turned to a pair of scissors as a substitute for the paintbrush, and continued his eminent career with no reversal whatever. When a business corporation such as General Electric closes a factory, employees usually have an option to move to another of its factories. But if the latter is geographically distant, then many employees may not really have that option and their occupational reversal can be drastic. Reversal could be negligible, however, if other companies eagerly wait to hire them because of their skills.

Also pertaining to the degree of severity of reversibility is the relativity of impact or attitudes toward reversals by those people involved in the passage. A heart attack may represent irreversible damage to all concerned. Or a minor success may be a good move

12. Orin Klapp, *Symbolic Leaders* (Chicago: Aldine Publishing Company, 1964).

forward by the agents while the passagees expecting great gains consider it a failure. Thus sociologically a move forward, but a minor distance, can be conceived of as a "comparative failure."[13] A demotion may, for instance, actually be welcomed by an executive who is tired of the grind, but it is seen as shameful by his peers.[14] Reversals that are fairly certain of being re-reversed may have relatively little impact on agents and passagees alike. All bide their time, say, through a case of flu. However, kinsmen of a terminal patient who is in a state of deterioration and pain usually are comforted when his end comes quickly; the extreme reversal is a blessing, albeit the less extreme was scarcely welcomed not many weeks before. Relative feeling about reversals, then, is occasioned by a combination of personal temperament, awareness of what actually is happening in the passage, general social values about what ought to be, and the structural context itself. The differential combined impact of these factors can easily cause differential relative variations in feelings about reversals by passagees, agents, and their witnesses.

The status passage that can be arrested or blocked is linked also to this relativity of reversibility. For some persons, the arrested passage may be merely a temporary respite rather than a genuine reversal. A student who leaves college to work for a year may consider this merely a respite from the rigors of academic work, whereas his parents or girlfriend may see him as a dropout who is undergoing a true reversal from a desired passage. In actuality neither may truly know, because as the phasing of the young man's work life continues, his arrested passage is likely to be redefined periodically. Because he begins very much to enjoy his work, he may wish to drop out of college for good, or as he prepares to return to college, his parents may see now that he really did take a respite. These redefinitions indicate that the relativity of reversals, and what they mean for those involved, are based on assumptions of what is a normal passage. The assumptions tend to vary, and more so when the passage and its transitional statuses lack clarity and codification.

13. Barney G. Glaser, "Comparative Failure in Science," *Science,* March 6, 1964, Vol. 143, pp. 1013-14.
14. Fred Goldner, "Demotion in Industrial Management," *American Sociological Review,* 30 (5) (October, 1965), pp. 714-24.

PERSONAL SOURCES OF REVERSIBILITY

The vital nature of status passages is that there are people involved — often continuously. These agents and passagees and their witnesses take into account each other and the structural conditions of the passage as they pursue their involvement. These actions become over time (or historically) *personal conditions* that can reverse the passage. For example, a personal condition in the dying passage is that most doctors decline to tell family members and a patient that he is dying. This condition results in the prevalent structural condition of a closed awareness context surrounding the unaware patient.[15] Patient and family anticipate recovery. Personal and structural conditions continuously interrelate and provide the explanations for where the passage is going, how fast, and why reversals may or do occur.[16]

A structural condition such as an hierarchy of authority may delegate more control over the passage to an agent than to a passagee; yet personal conditions intervene to explain how one uses his own, or undermines the other's control to reverse a status passage. The recalcitrant TB patient, who will not cooperate with his regimen, is setting up a personal condition to reverse his cure; he undermines the controls of the doctor designed to prevent reversals. If his noncompliance is discovered he may be kept in custody in a hospital to prevent his personal condition from interfering with a cure. Yet doctor and patient usually mutually cooperate during recovery passages to ward off reversals in the illness. Their cooperation involves avoiding personal conditions, such as working too hard, that may occasion a reversal.

When a patient or a doctor is noncooperative, and this personal condition portends a reversal, either may threaten the other to gain his cooperation. Linked with those more or less cooperative actions is the degree of awareness each has of the conditions of the passage, and how able and willing each is to cope with the conditions. *Such personal conditions limit the potential strategies that each may use to prevent or cause reversals.* The parolee and the parole agent who

15. A personal condition is a pattern of behavior of a party to the passage, say, the doctor's pattern of relating information on an illness to a patient. Personal conditions in aggregate become structural conditions; thus many doctors do not disclose terminality to patients, therefore nondisclosure is a structural condition of dying patients.

16. Glaser and Strauss, *Awareness.*

cannot or will not "play ball" with each other afford a good example of those limitations.

Agents in control have several resources for preventing reversals or causing them, if personally they wish to do this. They can control strategic information received by the passagee concerning how the passage is going, by blocking, distorting or misrepresenting the information. They can legitimate transitions in the passage to prevent reversals or to cause them. The true reasoning behind these actions need not be aired, if the agents are provided with the power to justify their actions in accord with accepted values or policy. Thus, a doctor taking his pediatric boards may be failed, when the true reasoning of a few doctors on the examining board is retribution for being refused membership in an institute to which the examinee belongs. People often wonder about the personal reason of an agent in preventing an expected reversal, such as a teacher promoting a child who does not merit it.

Because agents are often in control of many of the processes of a given passage, they can for personal reasons make phasing tough or easy for the passagee. If they make the beginning of a voluntary passage too tough, however, the passagee may quit in fear or disgust. Thus agents are limited in the degree of rigor they may apply to passages the passagee easily can leave or reverse. Where leaving is prohibited, agents can itensify any phase of the passage beyond where the passagee thinks it personally desirable. He has little or no recourse unless he can bring the agent's actions to the attention of a higher authority or appeal to some other structural constraint such as an operative ruling or law. Of course, he must be aware of these alternatives.

Intensifying rigors at the end of a leavable passage may cause reversals or dropouts that snatch imminent success from the passagee and his agent. So agents may lighten or shorten the end. It helps when the agent believes that the passagee has worked hard and also when the passagee's success is partly due to the agent, as in teaching. Again, if the passagee cannot drop out of passage of his own volition, he may find the end intensified, however not if the agents wish themselves to be remembered favorably afterward.

The agent's understanding and control of information, processes, and legitimation allows him to formulate strategies to prevent reversal that achieve a high degree of success. For example, the doctor will formulate a TB patient's regimen with respect to information, procedures, context of treatment, and conversion of the sputum test to insure against reversals caused by lack of conformity to the regimen. The doctor is less likely to allow the alcoholic or skid row patient to be left on his own in taking pills and may require the patient to visit the clinic at short intervals for pills or injections.[17]

Agents may also use their resources to prevent reversals by careful calculation of strategies which impinge on the passagee's identity as it derives from the passage. A reversal can cause an identity crisis if it smacks of failure. The agent can legitimate a potential failure as one of complete incompetence. However he may require retreading certain procedures or transitional statuses in case of reversal (such as requiring a student to start over if he misses too many basic classes) thereby trying to force the passagee to work harder to progress rather than face actual reversal. If the agent legitimates the reversal merely as a temporary setback and nothing to worry about ("it takes time to learn"), the passagee's identity is far less likely to be affected adversely from the reversal. The passagee may even seek it as a temporary respite from the rigors of the passage. Agents may encourage these respites with the hope that a refreshed passagee will move more quickly.

Moving on from one transitional status to another may also generate an identity crisis for a passagee who does not wish to move. For example, a scientist may resist being promoted to a higher position with a research organization because it entails more administrative work. Agents must calculate the use of their resources to prevent the passagee from reversing such a promotion. They may coach him through the change by simultaneously requiring that it occur.[18]

The degree to which a passagee can reverse his passage against agential wishes varies with their control and whether the reversals are deemed propitious. Even in the most agent-controlled of undesirable passages, however, the passagee is not without his resources, including escape or suicide.[19] Often he can engage in some action to reverse

17. Walter Klink, *Problems of Regimen Compliance in Tuberculosis* (Unpublished Ph.D. dissertation, Columbia University, 1969).

18. Anselm L. Strauss, *Mirrors and Masks* (San Francisco: The Sociology Press, 1970), pp. 100-31.

19. On "internal exile" see Mark G. Field, *Doctor and Patient in Soviet Russia,*

his passage while having ready a strategy to offset agents' efforts to re-reverse the passage. Patients can take placebos or store up narcotics for discretionary use. As the passagee's experience with a given passage increases, often his knowledge also grows concerning what resources are available to him for reversals, slowdowns, altering his passage directions, or by jumping to a passage that has a different direction. People engaged in organizational undesirable careers do this. They try to get their assignments changed or switch career lines. Even during wedding ceremonies, each passagee is given a voluntary out if he or she wishes, just before being pronounced married.

Passagees can easily occasion a reversal of an actually desirable passage by harboring inaccurate or distorted views of themselves or their passages. They may not understand the timing of the passage and goof up, as do students who miss an examination or who do not file papers on time. They also may have exaggerated views of their abilities or knowledge to cope with the passage at its next point, and because of their lack of preparation will fail temporarily until properly prepared. The passagee simply may not understand his agent's instructions and mistime the passage.

However, because passages are always changing, *misperceptions which are included in a range of real possibilities may not be permanently damaging. Re-reversals occur as correctives.* Once back on the track, moving again in the right direction, the passagee may come to realize his mistake and the circumstances that saved him, or he may continue to believe his misperception was correct and think he merely had some bad luck. His control agents, if there are some involved, probably will have a part in this appraisal, trying to guide him toward understanding what actually happened. This dialogue and its consequences must be based on empirical discovery, because agents also may misperceive. When differential misperceptions of agent and passagee is the prevailing condition there is less likelihood that a fairly accurate account will emerge.

Passagees often see ahead an undesirable reversal in their passage and decide to reverse earlier for different face-saving reasons while the "reversing is good." For example, apprentice jockeys who are not doing well in their riding tend to let their weight go up so that their

(Cambridge: Harvard University Press, 1957), Part II

advancement to becoming a jockey is blocked. Their reputations as riders are not hurt, their incompetence remains unknown. They cause the reversal to maintain a closed awareness context around the extent of their skill.[20]

Passagees may also decide literally to quit before involuntary reversal is thrust upon them — as with opera singers who have not quite made it to top stardom but whose voices are beginning to fail. Some occupations have inevitable reversals built into them so that passagees are advised by others to prepare for that eventuality. It is preferred that they have another occupation to move to when they must quit the present one. Airplane pilots and football players tend to invest in businesses as a hedge against the time they may be "washed out" by failing physical ability.

Investors also often decide to liquidate to cut current losses and prevent larger ones when the picture ahead looks bleak. Cutting losses becomes a small reversal but is justified as leading to a re-reversal because the passage otherwise is seen as proceeding steeply downward. If the passagee does not make such a redefinition — perhaps because he is in a closed awareness context (he lacks information) — then he may believe his investments are still going in the same upward direction and will wait out the small reversal as part of an expected cyclic pattern toward going up. Investors wait out dips in the stock market with confidence, not feeling that they are locked into a losing proposition. Investments are temporally conceived and thereby provide both definition of and interpretation for reversals.

There is a question, then, of whether a reversal is merely a phase of some re-reversal pattern of a passage that actually is continuing in the right direction over time or whether the reversal is real. This question pertains to the "shape" of the passage. The difficulty of answering will differ for clearly defined passages with re-reversal patterns or probably true reversals, as compared with unclearly defined passages where agent and passagee may make varied definitions with some justification.

Reversibility becomes quite complicated when one begins to conceptualize beyond a simple reversal and rereversal. Reversals can turn out to yield an arrested passage or to be a continuous passage in

20. Marvin Scott, *op. cit.*, Part 1.

another direction. Re-reversals can occur unexpectedly, or can expectedly occur so often that actually there exists a repeatable status passage — reversals, though expected, are also expected to be temporary. The student of status passages, while plotting their directions, must keep in mind the graphic direction of reverses; in doing this he will be seeing the passage as it occurs over *time. Direction and time result in the shape of a passage.*

3. TEMPORALITY

CONCERN about the direction of a status passage is closely linked with concern about its diverse temporal dimensions. Because a status passage is constantly in motion, the specifics of temporal concerns shift over time.[1]

People are interested in the temporal expectations for the passage as well as who is to legitimate and announce the expectations, and what differences in expectations will exist among participants in a passage. Also, what is the rate, pace, or speed of the passage, and how does it fluctuate in distance and direction? Is the rate scheduled or nonscheduled? What are the stages of passage or the transitional statuses, and are they prescribed sequences? Who is basically in control of the coordination or articulation of temporal aspects of the passage, particularly the movement between transitional statuses?

1. When combined, the two dimensions yield "the shape" of a status passage. That is, shape can be graphically shown on the two axes of time and direction. In the next chapter we consider the shaping of a passage.

Temporal Expectations And Legitimacy

Temporal expectations refer to any temporal aspects of status passage such as rate, transitional statuses, scheduling, or coordination. For example, a simple temporal expectation pertinent to the initial, transitional status of a heart attack — the period of seizure and pain — is how long a doctor may expect the patient to continue to cooperate with his efforts to promote recovery. This cooperation necessitates an intense, mutual, and continuous focus on one concern. As the seizure subsides and the patient devotes thought to his other concerns, *e.g.*, work, the doctor may expect the cooperation with treatment to lessen. When the pain passes entirely and recuperation starts, the next transitional status begins: the doctor then may have to use the threat of relapse or complete loss of life to keep the patient's cooperation. Thus the doctor paces his inducements for cooperation, basing them on temporal definitions and expectations of the case of chronic heart disease.

A main consideration of temporal expectations is: to what degree are they known with certainty? Obviously they can vary from completely known to completely unknown. This degree of certainty becomes a crucial condition for the people involved. They base much of their current behavior on their temporal expectations. For example, students will apply for jobs in July because they expect to get degrees in June. Many of us who temporally organize our passages throughout a day, are likely to minimize depending on those who refuse to do this because we fear delays, missed accomplishments, wasted time and lack of cooperation.

Accessibility to knowledge of temporal expectations is socially structured regarding determination and distributions when these expectations, as initiators of actions, are important to everybody. Within a given context or situation the person, who can legitimately determine temporal expectations and has discretionary power to withhold or announce them to others with some degree of clarity and of public noticeability, is generally known providing such an agent or passagee is designated or assumed. Thus, temporal expectations regarding a patient's illness legitimately can come only from the doctor, while those regarding an American engagement and marriage customarily come from the couple. In both cases others may pass on, if not initiate, the information. In both cases, also, the legitimators have discretionary power to generate the awareness context that surrounds the status passage.

When temporal expectations for a status passage are generally known, legitimators of timing, while necessary to making expectations official, are of less theoretical significance. This is because that to the degree the passage can be generally known to the public it can be scheduled, organized, and publicly announced for all who are interested. Then the legitimator simply becomes a part of the structure; he officially announces in approved, public ways the temporal aspects of the passage. For example, the registrar of a university publishes the official calendar for the school year, while other officials put out a calendar pertaining to his part in the student's passage. When the passage is thus organized because its temporal aspects must be sufficiently available to all people, the discretionary power of the legitimator is reduced. He is not so free to develop expectations or to decide how public to make them as is the legitimator of the private passages with unknown or indeterminate temporal expectations (the doctor on an illness or stock broker on an investment career).

Yet the organization for known expectations, which are made public, does not usually cover all temporal aspects of the passage. The organization is one of structural process, within which the yet unknown and diverse aspects of the passage may be conveniently either ignored or handled.[2] For example, every general hospital has organized a structural process to cope with the expectable temporal aspects of the surgical patient's status passage. That is, the structure of the hospital is in process to keep up with the patient's passage to recovery. He comes out of surgery and is immediately put in a recovery room near the operating room, so that if need be he can be rushed back to surgery. After a sufficient amount of time, usually several hours, he is put in an intensive care unit, which is arranged so that his vital signs can be watched closely, perhaps for several days, until he is out of danger. Then he is sent to the surgical floor to recuperate sufficiently to go home. This structural process in the hospital is set up to handle the known temporal aspects of recovery and some of the unknown

2. See Barney G. Glaser and Anselm L. Strauss, *Time for Dying* (Chicago: Aldine Publishing Company, 1968), Chapter 12.

ones — such as the emergency treatment of unexpected, quick reversals. The unknown aspects require a legitimator of the reversal and
of its temporal emergency and may not be publicized.

Still other unknown temporal relevancies may be completely
ignored and have no available official legitimators to handle them. If
the surgical patient has a midnight emergency, but the recovery room
is closed for lack of staff for a few hours, then the problem is where
to send the patient. Should he be left on the surgical floor until the
recovery room opens again or should he be sent to the ICU? If the
surgeon has gone, who is to legitimate how soon and where to send
the patient? Can a resident legitimate this move for a private patient?
Is the ICU set up to handle the surgical patient at this hour or is it
perhaps not adequately staffed during this early morning hour? Differential expectations of potential legitimators abound. In sum, even the
most structually organized of status passages can become quite problematic, when the structural process cannot temporally keep up with
or be modified to handle the passage. Legitimators then become crucial for temporal handling of the passage in ways that break through
an organizational mold. Of three patients simultaneously starting to
die, which one will receive the full effort of an ICU staff depends in
part on the doctor or nurses in charge who juggle priorities in care,
as based on their temporal expectations concerning which patient
needs immediate attention the most. Emergency wards and ICU's are
organized for intense quick care — but in accordance with who can
wait and who cannot.

*When temporal aspects are generally unknown or must be created
arbitrarily anew, legitimators and their announcements are of great
theoretical significance.* [3] When legitimators must establish temporal
expectations, behavior and *ad hoc* organization based on these expectations will emerge. Hence to forestall either behaviors he does not
want from others or behaviors based on too uncertain a timing, the

3. "There is usually in each tribe a man whose privilege it is to open and close
initiation periods and to give each (age) set its name. This man belongs to one of those
lineages which have a special ritual relationship to cattle and are known as 'Men of the
Cattle.' He opens and closes initiation periods in his own district, and other districts
of his tribe follow suit. Once a period has been opened, each village and district initiates
its boys when it pleases." E.E. Evans-Pritchard, "The Nuer of the Southern Sudan"
in M. Fortes and E.E. Evans-Pritchard, *African Political Systems* (London: Oxford
University Press, 1940), p. 289.

legitimator, whether agent or passagee, may hesitate to announce any expectation. He may generate a closed awareness context so that all wait and see, as in the uncertain rescue of trapped miners when official proclamations tell of possible progress while time drags on for the families. Agents who work on the "wait and see" passage are thereby allowed to work in a temporal vacuum. Sometimes, irrespective of unknown timing, they may be under pressure to work fast because of the untoward direction of the passage — disaster or death is imminent. Otherwise they can work at their own pace under no pressure when the direction does not justify a special rate of passage.

Sometimes the legitimator announces a timing even when unknown, if others will stick to the passage only when a timing is created.[4] He may tentatively *estimate time* as based on his knowledge of other cases, and will ask people to be alert for reversals and delays and not pin all their behavior on his temporal expectations for the particular passage. The secondary school teacher is in this position when pressed by parents about when their child will learn to read well. Or the legitimator may *promise time,* as when a revolutionary leader, to keep discouraged followers going, offers a timetable for the next step of the revolution.

Promised time is crucial because the legitimator has a structural prerogative to create a timing for the passage by which others may (even should) then organize their behavior for its duration. Much work is organized around promised time, as the example of revolutionists suggests. Likewise, the TB patient and nurses organize their behavior in regard to the patient's illness on the promised timing of the doctor who originally set up the treatment regimen. Building contractors promise each installation stage of plumbing and wiring at certain times, so the builder can arrange timing for funds and other subcontractors as the building passage progresses.

In promising time the legitimator may have one or several goals. Not really knowing, he may simply promise any time just to get the passagee and other agents working, for he reckons getting people in motion is the most important task at the moment. Also he expects that when the others realize the timing is off, their tolerance and experience will lead to adjustments so as to pick up the slack in his erroneous

4. Dorothy Miller, "County Lunacy Commission Hearings," *Social Problems,* Vol. 14, 1966.

timing, so the sentimental order surrounding the work is not too jolted.

Sometimes the legitimator knows the true timing but realizes that, if revealed, others would not work or not work with him — so he promises what they wish to hear. He is then fully prepared to ignore his temporal commitment and to time the work as best fits the evolving passage, which he watches closely. Subcontractors, architects, moving men, doctors, and lawyers continually do this to initiate clients' passages and to retain clients. When the legitimator's timing does not pan out, the sentimental order of those involved in a passage may be jarred and severe acrimony may result. However, if the legitimator can explain, hold things together and retain enough control to pull off the passage, everyone may become happy again even if things dragged or happened too quickly. With doctors, lawyers, and subcontractors usually the passage is replete with delays and sometimes with reversals.

The legitimator, of course, can sincerely promise a timing he expects everyone, including himself, to follow. If his timing proves to be off, he suffers from a sense of failure in responsibility, and he may incur disrespect and distrust and may have trouble retiming the passage for others. His own sentiments, as well as the sentimental order among those who expected accordance with his timing, can be severely upset. However, the others may cheerfully help him resolve his mistake as he offers new timing, if they reason that under such unknown circumstances any person is liable to err. How they respond depends on conditions such as the centrality of the passage to them, whether reversals are involved, and the degree of the empathy of others.

Another condition that affects others' responses to maltiming by a legitimator is their experience with the type of passage. If inexperienced, they are likely to feel "conned" or "taken for fools." The legitimator is then liable to find it difficult to redress their feelings, save with the most naive who remain devoted to his authority, despite the negative consequences of his maltiming. Yet experienced people tend to realize the low probability or impossiblity of accurately predicting the distant future, and therefore accept promised time simply as a means for initiating the passage. They try not to associate with legitimators whom they believe are incapable of handling timing as it emerges during an evolving passage. ("Yes, I believe the doctor when he says he can do this. I have trust in him, but when he says that I will be ready in three weeks, I don't believe him at all," said an experienced patient. A builder said, "I go along with anything 'X' [a plumber] says knowing that he'll watch and when it's time to be on the job he won't fail me.") Experience tempers credibility about promised time, while increasing tolerance for unfulfilled expectations. Experienced agents and passagees can more easily discount poor timing and keep up the passage or know when to quit. Experience means that it is less necessary to keep the awareness context closed on timing and more difficult for the legitimator to do so if he tries.

The legitimator who must create a timing for a seldom tried, new, or temporally unknown passage has more discretion in setting the timing than has a legitimator for a passage wherein the timing is generally well known, and typically scheduled and organized — e.g. a school year. The latter legitimator must usuaily clear changes with others who are involved in organizing the passage. They limit his discretion even when he has power to make changes. The legitimator, who must create timing for a relatively new or temporally unknown passage, is limited only by the nature of the situation and by the experience of others in this type of passage, who are also directly linked to the awareness context in which he creates the timing.

For example, the policeman on the beat has considerable discretionary power on whether *to start* a person who is potentially or actually mentally ill through a passage to a mental hospital.[5] If the person is a public nuisance or a danger or a burden to his family, the awareness context relative to his illness is open, and the policeman's discretion is limited to how long he can let him be troublesome before others require him to be taken into custody. If the awareness context is relatively closed (perhaps nobody or only one family member knowing of the illness), the policeman can more easily afford to wait to see if the person becomes a public liability. The policeman usually will prefer this slower "wait and see" timing to give the ill person (or others) time to manage restraint to avoid putting the person through the apprehension process and to avoid work for himself in following the ill person through all processing. Sometimes the family will pro-

5. Egon Bittner, "Police Discretion in Emergency Apprehension of Mentally Ill Persons," *Social Problems* (Winter, 1967) Vol. 14, No. 3, pp. 278-93.

vide a protective shield to give the ill kinsman time to reverse his illness passage.

In slowing down the timing as much as possible to allow a person to avoid the apprehension and incarceration passage, the policeman, as a legitimator, uses criteria pertaining to the harm the person may be to himself or others. If the policeman brings the offender into passage, its temporal aspects become highly organized, and the policeman's temporal discretion disappears. The temporal organization of apprehension and incarceration processes provides a whole succession of legitimators concerned with time and duration. The offender is brought before a judge who must decide whether to hold the person on a 72 – hour observation, and the judge uses medical advisers to appraise the person's condition. As these people choose his direction, the temporal aspects of his passage fall in line. For instance, they may decide that he be kept under observation before commitment.

The legitimator who must render timing as it actually emerges also has more discretion than the legitimator of an already organized passage. Although the former's timing supposedly is based on reading cues, as he anticipates further events with discretion he can, if accepted as an expert, create the timing as he sees it. Again, doctors and lawyers are in this position. Though expected to be the legitimate readers of emergent timing of a client's passage, in fact they use their authority to create, as much as read, the timing. When a woman is in labor, the doctor watches her closely to determine when the baby will be born to have her inside the delivery room in ample time. But, in fact, he may read the cues differently than the nurses and appear to them to create a timing that is not emergent. Or, because of certain of her physical problems or his commitments elsewhere, he may have the patient sent to the delivery room apparently ahead of schedule and there induce a faster delivery. In reverse, lawyers are master craftsmen at creating delays which are based on the emergent timing of clients' passages through law suits or prosecutions.

Rate and Schedule of Passage

The rate of a passage is closely linked with its scheduling. As we have said, passages with known temporal expectations tend to be organized, and this organization usually provides a schedule for the passage. In turn, this schedule indicates the speed of the passage by which agents and passagees pace themselves and by which they claim delays and speedups.

The rate of a passage is of deep concern to agents and passagees because they wish to know not only where they are going (direction) but approximately how soon they will arrive there. A scheduled passage, of course, provides the best temporal expectations. Knowing its scheduled rate, people can choose a passage and make legitimate demands with reference to the schedule when delays or speed-ups occur. Because many passages are not too well scheduled, or not scheduled at all (because, as we have seen, unknown temporal expectations must emerge or be created in passage) rates, pacing, and delays become theoretically significant problems.

The scheduled passage sets forth how the person is moved along at a *prescribed rate* by indicating the number of transitional statuses, in what order or sequence they fall, and how long the person will be in each transitional status. Passage through public school is a classical example. Rate of passage can be counted upon unless the student skips, is held back, or demoted. A high degree of scheduling allows temporal linkage to the passage of prescribed, public ceremonies (graduation) and of personal ceremonies (a dinner celebration).

Even if people do not wish ceremonies, the temporal mechanics of a highly scheduled passage may put or force them through the ceremony — on time — just as through the passage itself. The "mechanical" or "ritualistic" elements may personally leave many an agent and passagee with little concern for the ceremony. Their reactions may, however, vary not only according to personal tastes but according to type and stage of ceremony; for instance, passage through a transitional status versus through the final step. Closure — a strategic temporal variable — usually tends to be more important. Thus, a closure ceremony which signifies an end to the passage (graduation) usually is of more concern than most transitions. However, if the passage was very difficult or indicates a significant advance (in the life cycle a transition from boyhood to manhood, for example), a transitional ceremony may be of great concern even though only a part of some longer highly scheduled passage.

A closure ceremony for the slightly scheduled or nonscheduled passage also is of much concern to participants, because closure may be the only certain temporal aspect of the passage. Slight scheduling or nonscheduling means that people may not really be sure of closure until the passage is capped with a ceremony. This is especially so for passages whose beginning and transitions in large degree occur in a closed awareness context. The marriage ceremony usually is important and less important, but perhaps still of much concern, is the transition ceremony leading to a somewhat publicized engagement such as an engagement party, a ceremonial viewing of a ring, or a passing the ring ceremony among student nurses.[6] These socially structured occasions mark a temporal change in the transitional status of dating to that of being engaged, in what usually is an otherwise unscheduled, closed awareness context passage to marriage. When a transitional point, however, is of not much concern for the people involved it can easily be passed over, because the passagees acting as their own agents require no ceremony — at least no public one.

Highly scheduled passages, characterized by rates that do not require constant, quick action, generate conditions for the development of rituals designed to get passage work done on time or early.[7] This development forestalls disruption both to the work and to the sentimental order of a passage. Thus, students study ahead of time for an exam; police drive through their beats quickly and then with their radio on sleep parked under overpasses. Early rituals allow agents and passagees to relax so that they can later meet a schedule on time without pressure. But when agents force passagees into early rituals, they can become very restless waiting too early for the next step. Soldiers, especially trainees and combat soldiers, are typically brought places ahead of schedule and get restless or bored while waiting for action.

Early rituals may also develop for nonscheduled passages, even when their directions and ends are uncertain. Thus a possible, but not certain moribund patient may be administered last rites or told to take leave of a relative who has travelled from afar and will return home, just in case the patient might die quickly. The early ritual (which may

    6. Fred Davis, "Rituals of Annunciation Marrying Among Student Nurses," in Jack Douglas (Ed.), *Existential Sociology,* forthcoming.
    7. Joseph R. Gusfield, "Moral Passage: The Symbolic Process in Public Designations of Deviance," *Social Problems,* Vol. 15, No. 2, Fall 1967, pp. 175-188.

be a full fledged ceremony as are the last rites) occurs under the assumption that it is better to be ahead of time with an action than too late or not at all.

The initiators of early rituals tend to neglect the consequence of wasted time and unfavorable consequences from opening up a closed awareness context before it is either scheduled or advisable to be opened (an early ritual signaling to a patient that he will die can speed up the death). These early rituals are initiated by agents and passagees who wish to relieve themselves of the pressure of being late, whatever its source may be. Pressure arises because the scheduled passage typically has clear negative sanctions linked to it to prevent delays and positive sanctions to encourage promptness. Delays, speedups, and pacing are less problematic regarding sanctions for nonscheduled passages, because of lacking the rigidity or reference of the schedule and its rate of passage. In nonscheduled passages the issues regarding certainty become more problematic. The pressure in nonscheduled passages comes from the desire to relieve the uncertainty about when to get important things done before it is too late. Questions of delay, speed-up and pacing revolve around trying to establish schedules that have some certainty of temporal expectation. A classic example is the broker trying to pace the passage of an inexperienced client into the status of investor in the highly nonscheduled stock market. He does not wish to miss readiness phases, so he takes early chances rather than lose his chance altogether.

The temporal problems of ceremonies, early rituals, delays, speedups, and pacing are supported by the sentimental order of the status passage. By sentimental order we mean that people involved in the passage will have feelings that things will happen according to temporal expectations. The more these expectations are scheduled, the stronger the feelings of expectation, and the more disquieting are unfulfilled expectations.

Temporal changes, such as delays, reversals which cause delays and poor pacing — a teacher does not get her class through a full year's work within the stated year — *are disruptive of this sentimental order.* Because the threats to this sentimental order — which underwrites the temporal order — can be disastrous, knowledgeable agents or passagees may wish to keep potential or actual temporal changes within a closed awareness context as long as possible. Possible failures due to delay or changes are covered up, while the agents or passagees work feverishly to catch up. If they do not and the word gets out, other participants become very upset. The negative consequences deriving from a disrupted sentimental order of a scheduled passage usually are guarded against — or postponed — as much as possible.

When the passage is not too well scheduled, or even mainly nonscheduled, the sentimental order which takes into account temporal unknowns is not so threatened by temporal changes. Even undesirable changes that result in severe reversals may be received more tolerantly because of the temporal unknown. For example, a young man went to school in Colorado to make the ski team. In practicing for his tryouts he broke his leg, and he knew he could not make the team until the following year, but he and his family were not too upset because he might not have made it anyway.

Not only is tolerance for delays and malpacing part of the sentimental order of a nonscheduled passage, but this tolerance feeds into the sentiment that timings, etc. are more readily negotiable than in the scheduled passage. As the temporality of any aspect of the nonscheduled passage emerges or is created, usually those involved tend to negotiate it; so their actions during the passage will be articulated around, minimizing delays. They set suitable rates and decide who paces the passage and when. In essence, these negotiations institute mini-schedules (over the knowns) of the passage. These notions are typical of a patient's illness career in hospitals and mental institutions,[8] and in unstructured organizational careers where people mini-schedule their careers while waiting for the movement of others before they are considered for promotion.[9]

These negotiations over mini-schedules also apply to non-scheduled passages that can only be broadly scheduled because of many temporal unknowns. This phenomenon occurs in on-the-job training programs, where the students are given a certain number of weeks in which to learn a skill or job. It is also characteristic of advanced graduate schooling and of the novel programs of ungraded

8. Glaser and Strauss, *op. cit.;* Erving Goffman, *Asylums* (Chicago: Aldine Publishing Company, 1961). "The Underlife of a Public Institution," pp. 171-320. Kathy Calkins, "Institutional Time: Perspectives, Marking and Management," *Social Problems* (Spring, 1970).

9. See Barney G. Glaser (Ed.) *Organizational Careers* (Chicago: Aldine Publishing Company, 1968); see articles on promotion, demotion, and succession. pp. 191, 375.

primary and secondary schools.[10] The broad schedule applies to beginning and ending dates which enclose a period of nonscheduled training.

The sentimental order supports the rate, fluidity, and flexibility of such passages with regard to establishing their timing; in so doing it supports the increasingly open awareness fostered by negotiation. Closed awareness contexts are due to a yet unknown temporality rather than to concerted efforts at concealing schedules and rates. Only an official legitimator, who may wish to keep secret an emerging schedule, has the power to do so by interpreting the temporal expectations "his way" rather than as they actually emerge. Doctors often do this with chronically ill or dying patients. They may "fudge" during the temporal negotiations to keep the patient unaware of an impending decline or worsening of symptoms. Yet, so strong is the sentimental order supporting the true temporal expectations as they are realized that, within such closed contexts, a doctor's misrepresentations are hard to maintain. A family member or a nurse can easily give away the truth by manner, inflection, or slip.

The negotiated mini-schedule brings forth the problem of pacing the passage. For the brief span covered by the mini-schedule in the nonscheduled passage, the agents and passagees have a rate by which to pace their work. Problems of pacing delays, speed-ups, etc. emerge as with the scheduled passage but within a cushion of nonscheduled time that picks up the temporal spill-overs from slack of early rituals and delays. The agents or passagees are not robbing time or being late or missing or beginning something new. Such temporal leeway is characteristic of the passage through courtship-engagement-marriage, as the couple sets up mini-schedules along an unknown temporal span that progresses toward family life. Unknown blocks of time cushion their attempts at putting transitions on schedule. Authors tend to mini-schedule themselves for daily periods of writing, which they negotiate with their family, during the temporally unknown passage of writing a book.

Another example is the pacing by hospital nurses of kinsman visits to a very sick patient. During the unknown illness career there are scheduled visiting hours that bracket the relatively few minutes

10. See Ethel Ruymaker, *Sorting Processes in Elementary School* (Unpublished Ph.D. Dissertation, University of California, Berkeley, 1970).

family members may spend with the patient. As the nurse paces these short visits made during the visiting hours, she can delay or prolong the visit, make people take turns, or hurry up their visit. On both sides of the visit there is the temporal cushion of the visiting hours. Delays are not too bothersome to the visitor or patient unless visiting hours are over, forcing a postponed visit. However, being hurried or ushered out too soon can be felt as unfair unless either the visiting hours are over (the bracket condition), or the patient's physical condition clearly prevents an extended visit. In some cases the nurse can ignore the end of visiting hours and prolong the visit if conditions warrant it.

Sometimes mini-schedules that are set up for a temporally unknown passage can foster the wrong pacing wherein the control agents mistakenly assume a temporal cushion after the schedule and then discover that none exists. When the discovery is too late, consequences can be drastic, but more often the passagee is likely to be quite disturbed by the lack of temporal leeway and by the delay. The cardiac patient who is thought to be out of danger may be left to sleep til morning and suffer a reversal (a heart attack) requiring immediate emergency care. He is in trouble because the staff thinks they have until morning before resuming additional care. Letting him sleep amounts to a temporal cushion. The patient must, if he can, signal the new attack, or he may die for lack of care, in the very context set up for people to be watched constantly for immediate emergency care when, however, it is expected that no temporal cushion exists.

Emergency systems are temporally set up to handle passages where agents or passagees think they have a temporal cushion yet are still wary of malpacing themselves. In learning to be in the stock market as an investor, a person may believe he has time to think about selling a stock or to get advice from his broker, but if the market drops suddenly he may have no time. He is taught by the broker how to cover his passage through investments with stop-loss orders — automatic sells at a specific price — to cover potential quick loss of expected temporal cushions in such a temporally hazardous, unknown passage. Learning to be a good investor puts a premium on learning skills to pace one's portfolio, hence oneself, through the market. Because this pacing is tricky and difficult even to mini-schedule, brokers stand ready with information, sell orders, and averaging techniques to build temporal cushions into a portfolio at the slightest hint of malpacing of expected cushions. Delays — so to speak — are almost non-existent in pacing because scheduling is so difficult. What is prevalent is working the market either too fast or too slow, risking losing a cushion and forcing one to repace himself.

Transitional Statuses

It is important that we continue to see a status passage temporally rather than statically. *The passagee is in constant movement over time, not just "in" a status.* To aid in this conceptualization we must think of temporal social structures — that is social structures in continuous process — and of their processual aspects. One such aid is the concept of *transitional status.*

If we ask how a social system in process keeps a person in passage between two statuses for a period of time, the answer is: *He is put into a transitional status or a sequence of them, which helps account in large measure for the period of time he will be in passage and the sequences of transitions.* If the status passage is scheduled, then its transitional statuses will denote how much time he will be in them and what is their sequence. The army recruit, for example, is slated to spend eight weeks in basic training as a trainee in his passage from civilian to soldier. For unscheduled passages, transitional statuses refer to the sequence of transitions with probabilities of how much time each transition may or should take under certain conditions.

Some passages do not have clearly delineated transitional statuses; then the entire passage is seen as a transition, until transitional statuses are delineated or emerge. For example, becoming a marijuana user originally was seen as a transition, but further study showed it has several transitional statues of which the agents were aware.[11]

Further, although some transitional statuses encumber only on a certain dimension of the passagee's existence, they may require that his total existence occur in a particular context. A mental patient may require therapy a few times a week; the rest of the time other aspects of his life are prominent, and his illness is subordinate. Thus, his illness passage is attended to only intermittently. Yet, if its manifesta-

---

11. Howard S. Becker, "Becoming a Marihuana User," in *Outsiders* (New York: The Free Press, 1963) pp. 41-58.

tions are too disruptive to others and his other passages, the patient may have to be kept in custody because even during the short time that his illness is dominant it makes him a social and self control problem. In custody, transitions may be controlled more effectively. Of course, custody renders the patient less opportunity for engaging in other passages. Organizational careers which require "9 to 5" attendance also constrain freedom for other passages during the eight hours, although a man may not really be working all this time.

We must be cognizant both of the *length of time which a transition takes and the time the passagee must devote to this transition.* A transition may last a certain length of time, such as eight weeks of basic traning or the 72-hour hold on a mental patient. In both instances, the time devoted to the transition is virtually 100 per cent. Whether these transitions are considered long or short is a consideration relative to the passagee's context and to his other passages. If the basic trainee is whisked off to war he may feel the training was too short!

Some transitions may require the passagee to devote only intermittent short amounts of time while the transitional status goes on a long time — such as in becoming an investor, driver, or a marijuana user. These transitions easily allow the passagee to undertake other passages at the same time. Night-school courses, which are designed to train people for new careers, have institutionalized this flexibility, allowing an intermittent devotion to transitional statuses.

This example suggests also that *passages may require time during a part of the day which is usually untouched by other passages.* Policemen can moonlight other jobs during the day. Mothers of school children are free to work or study daily from 9:00 to 3:00 PM. Transitional statuses, by structuring the time required to be devoted to the passage, allow us to formulate the notions needed to understand a person's multiple status passages (a topic discussed at length in Chapter 7).

The intermittency of transitional statuses points up two other important properties. One is that *the degree of intermittency sets forth whether communication between a passagee and his agent(s) is usually continuous or intermittent.* Usually they vary together. Thus if a passagee who is engaged in an intermittent, transitional status wishes continually to talk to his agent, this activity may prove very disruptive to the passage because they will communicate when the passage is temporally dormant. Generally this break of temporality is accepted only during an emergency. Thus, a patient knows he cannot continually speak with his doctor unless an emergency warrants it; the routine communications are reserved for their next meeting. However, when a transitional status requires relatively continuous communication, intermittent periods of respite will occur so that passagee and agent do not become exhausted nor exasperated with one another. The lulls control an otherwise complete mutual accessibility. Thus honeymooners cannot continually talk, nor can a piano student and his coach.

The second property which marks degree of intermittency of transitional statuses is the differential contribution of time made by agent and passagee to the passage. Passages requiring continuous devotion to a transition by the passagee will, in all likelihood, be marked by a great disparity of time put into it by the agent. A post-surgical patient will devote far more time to his recovery than his doctor.[12] Recuperating from virtually any disease offers the same condition of disparity. When the *transitional status becomes more intermittent, parity of time is likely to be more equal between agent and passagee.* Thus student and teacher or psychiatrist and patient meet each week for a certain amount of time. Preparation for meetings will make the difference. Sometimes the passagee and sometimes the agent devotes more time to preparation depending on the stage of the passage. Elementary school teachers ordinarily prepare more for class than do their students, as may a surgeon before an operation if it is a very difficult or unusual one. Of course, graduate students spend more time than their advisors preparing for meetings.

Equal time is devoted to a transition also when passagees or agents experience a sustained interest in each other or in the outcome of the passage. Two passagees — engaged persons, for example — may work together very hard. Swimming coaches and their favored athletes tend to work hard together at practice attempting to perfect the latter's skills.

The complaints and annoyances over the disparity of time that is devoted to transitions commonly are voiced by either agents or passagees: "He isn't doing his share." These complaints are increased

12. Walter Klink, *Problems of Regimen Compliance in Tuberculosis* (Unpublished Ph.D. Dissertation, Columbia University, 1969).

when one party defines the current transitional status as demanding much more mutual working together than does the other. Hence, lags in temporal definitions occur when, say, an agent thinks the passage now needs less attention and time than before, while the passagee does not see or agree to the new phase. These lags are likely to lead to strain between agent and passagee and to the necessity to renegotiate these relationships, or dissolve them, or suffer the consequence of continued strain.

The sequences, implied in the notion of transitional status, allow planning for changes in temporal requirements. Again, this planning affects the temporal flexibility of the passagee. By knowing when his transition ends and the conditions for his next transition, he knows in which other passages he may engage and when they must end. For instance, the basic army trainee will know approximately when he is to be transferred overseas and how long a tour of duty is. Thus he can adjust the temporal requirements of the particular passage to his other passages and vice versa.

The sequential order of transitional statuses allows passagees and agents to plan ahead for the next transition, or for the actual end of the status passage. *In planning ahead they focus on at least two consequences of transitions. One is to minimize the shock or depression that may otherwise in some degree often follow the transition.* This is illustrated by the depression students often feel after taking an exam for which they have worked very hard. The "let down" can be very deflating, when the buildup was strong over a period of time.[13] A mother's postpartum depression is another example of the same phenomenon.

A second focus in planning is to make certain the next transition or status passage is desirable. This is illustrated by retirement and by the changing of careers. In making a break with a passage or ending it, the letdown is almost sure to come. This is minimized by planning ahead for a new, desirable passage. Some writers, artists, and scientists avoid this letdown — having learned through experience — by beginning a piece of new work long before ending an old one so the change may even go unnoticed or be welcomed.

Ending a major passage, such as an occupational career, requires

13. Virginia L. Olesen and Elvi W. Whittaker, *The Silent Dialogue* (San Francisco: Jossey-Bass, Inc., 1968); see references on emotional cycles.

planning ahead on several important dimensions. New equilibriums must be worked out for finances, work, and social life. These equilibriums hopefully offer continuity to the person's life, although some shock nevertheless may occur because of reduced financial capacity. At any rate, minimizing or preventing reversals in style of life is the goal of this kind of planning.

Many people have a tendency to *overplan,* especially when the coming transition seems destined to be very stressful. When someone is slowly dying from cancer, family members prepare themselves and each other, both as agents in the dying passage, and as passagees themselves to widowhood or to childlessness. They may plan ahead so well that they are quite "grieved out" before the death — and sometimes, as a result, the dying person is left to rather lonely last days. His death brings relatively little shock, making his kinsmen look rather callous to others. Another consequence of overplanning may be disruption of the current transition because too much work is devoted to the next transitional status. Thus graduate students often let the last semester's work slide, while looking for a job for after graduation, and medical students and residents are virtually "out of school" during the late spring as they plan for and dream about their oncoming internships and practices.[14]

In contrast, people also tend to *underplan* for the next transitional status because of several other reasons. The schedule for the transition is unknown because there is none, the transition is new for the people involved, or there is a closed awareness context with regard to the schedule. Sometimes the next transitional sequence is not even known, for the same reasons, therefore what to plan for is problematic. Also, unscheduled transitional statuses can appear so fast that people are caught unaware or appear so slowly that people forget they are in transition and are surprised when the passage ends. Still other people are not motivated to plan ahead because they hope matters will take care of themselves or because the next transition is undesirable. Some deny a current transition and thereby constrain planning for the future. Some feel whatever is planned for them is unavoidable so why fight it?

There are agents who make a profession of managing transitions

14. Howard S. Becker *et al, Boys in White* (Chicago: University of Chicago Press, 1961), pp. 384-400.

to get passagees "through without any bruises." Doctors, lawyers, nurses, social workers, architects, counselors, and others in the practicing professions see this as one of their many tasks as they help shape clients' passages. They see sections of passages as rough and conceive of themselves as experts who are ever alert to unknown contingencies with consequences that can be softened. Some passagees, aware that such ability exists, will look within their price range for the "best man in town" to help ensure transitions which will occur with a minimum of stress. They need to feel their agents are the best. Poorly qualified or unskilled agents can make the passage needlessly rough.

One special type of sequence in transitional statuses is the organizational career. This can be highly routinized — as in the civil service — so that an organizational career can be planned ahead for years, each transition scheduled with care. When organizational succession is not routinized, planning is usually confined to strategies for getting an appointment to the next opening whenever it might appear. This opening is linked with the careers of other people in the organization, so figuring out the interdependence of those careers is the first job of the passagee and his sponsors, if he has any.[15] Once figured out, appropriate strategies follow. Planning here amounts to "making it," as one hears about it in the competitive governmental, academic, and business world.

Temporal Articulation

Temporal articulation of a status passage refers to a single passage, to multiple passages of one person, and to the number of people going through each passage and how those people are related — whether, for instance, the passages are solo, aggregate, or collective. Here we discuss some of the basics of articulating one passage: in Chapters 7 and 6 we shall take up, respectively, multiple articulation, and the articulation problems of aggregate and collective passages.

By the temporal articulation is meant the pacing of a passagee

15. Alvin W. Gouldner, "The Problem of Succession in Bureaucracy," in Alvin W. Gouldner (Ed.) *Studies in Leadership* (New York: Harper, 1950), pp. 339-451; Bernard Levenson, "Bureaucratic Succession," in Amitai Etzioni (Ed.) *Complex Organizations* (New York: Holdt Rinehart, Winston, 1961), pp. 362-75.

through the passage according more or less to the clarity of the scheduling and of the transitional statuses. Either the passagee or agents may be in control of such pacing. Temporal articulation is based on the general priority of work over the sentimental order of a passage. When work is too early or too late, the sentimental order is disrupted through reactions to the malpacing of the passage. Then complaints of passagees or agents may raise the priority of sentiments to the level of work or beyond it. These sentiments must be taken care of, whether by adjusting the work or by successful efforts to mollify the upset. Large organizations have public relations bureaus to mollify clients who are irate over malpacing, irrespective of whether the passage is thereby brought back into proper temporal articulation. Usually the modification is directed toward helping the passagee to put up with delays. Most agents expect to mollify sentiments as part of their work at temporal articulation. Passagees also can mollify themselves. As we have said, the less scheduled a passage the more easily malpacing occurs, but then people are more tolerant of disruptions to the work and sentimental orders. Tolerance is based on lack of certainty of temporal expectations, so unfulfilled ones are less disappointing, and lack of clear signs of malpacing makes awareness of it harder and therefore easier to conceal.

The negative consequences of disrupted work and sentimental orders during a status passage lead to early rituals, promised time, lead time effort, notification processes, planning ahead, scheduling, and so forth to ensure continuous articulation of the passage. These efforts may all be conceived of as the *prearticulation of a passage* — which occurs as much as possible so as to minimize potential disarticulation. Temporal disarticulation may occur from blockages or reversals in the passages due to sickness, failure, exhaustion, stupidity, lack of skill on the part of agent or passagee. Prearticulation tries to prevent these sources of disarticulation from occurring or having much effect.

When delay is the source of disarticulation, the passage may continue on without the passagee or slow down or stop to wait for him. Each alternative can lead to negative consequences. If the passage continues, then the passagee must either start over or forget the passage and perhaps find a new one. Specific conditions will decide whether he is forced to start over. If sickness prevents a person from continuing basic training for the military service, he may have to start anew with a different training unit because his original company goes on without him. If somebody falls behind at school because of illness, he may have to start over because of compulsory education, or in college he may choose a new course or quit school. Being left behind is usually quite disruptive to a person's sentiments and to his agents. It can, however, be seen as a way out of a "bad" passage for all concerned.

The schedule for others involved in a passage that is stopped for a delay by an agent or passagee is ruined, and the passage itself may be harmed. Stopping also has negative effects for other persons' passages. For example, if a main actor does not appear for rehearsal, progress toward a finished performance is hindered for all concerned and others may become quite upset, fearing the play will not open on schedule and other commitments may be delayed.

Because of this threat of hurting others or the passage itself through the failure of one person, various covering strategies develop to prevent disarticulations that might block or reverse a passage. Schools or private teachers arrange for substitute teachers, and theatrical productions provide for understudies for the principal performers in the show. These substitutes are "on call," so that in an emergency nothing much is lost even if the quality or distance covered is slowed down.

Passages, then, that slow down because of disarticulation may be the result of substitute agents or passagees acting to prevent a complete blockage. Often passages will be slowed down, however, because of the reduced capacity of an agent or passagee to work on it. The sources of this may be, for example, a personal problem, or becoming drawn elsewhere, or having other demands made on one's time. The context in which the passage occurs may slow it down, as when a research project is slowed because of cutbacks in financing. The natural tendency in a slowdown, whatever the source, is for a passagee or agent to go over the head of the person accountable to seek a resolution by a person who has authority to increase the pace of the passage. When an organization of agents is involved, one can go to a superior to get more action out of the particular lower level agent who is slowing down the passage. This strategy is found frequently within organizations — whether government or business — ("I want to see the manager!").

Sometimes a passagee who uses this strategy discovers that lesser agents are delaying because a higher level agent did not leave temporally defined orders for moving the passage along. Thus, it is not unusual for a patient who has just been admitted to a hospital to be denied painkilling drugs for several hours by a nurse until his doctor can be reached. In this instance the temporal organization of a hierarchy of agents is disarticulated — in turn this leads to disarticulation of the passage. A loudly moaning patient in great pain disrupts the sentimental order of the ward, despite his attempts to control himself.

Disarticulation from speedups in the timing of a passage by a passagee or agent can also be disruptive to work and sentimental orders. If one person is allowed to change the timing, others — passagees and agents alike — may become demoralized by a pace with which they cannot keep up. If an agent or passagee is more than slightly held back, waiting for others to catch up so that the passage can proceed, he becomes restless, annoyed, bored and perhaps gives up. These situations are illustrated in the classroom by students who cannot keep up with the pace setters and by quick students who must wait for slower classmates to catch up. Several strategies have been developed to cope with such potential disarticulations in students' passages. Fast students are given extra work or are enlisted as teacher helpers as a way of passing the extra time while waiting for the rest of a class to catch up. Teachers who cannot stand slow classes seek schools or classes whose pace satisfies them. Schools develop special classes for slow and gifted groups or programs of team teaching and individual direction as attempts to handle malpacing problems.

One area for strategies in preventing slowdowns — and a condition for causing them if the strategy malfunctions — is in the managing of temporal expectations involved in coordinating the passage. Either the agent or passagee may employ this strategy. Because parties to the passage adjust their behavior according to temporal definitions, the coordination of these expectations is crucial for all so that they work sufficiently well together. At least one party must know both how to time the passage and how others are timing it. In a building project, for example, the general contractor has the responsibility to make certain everyone knows what they need to know at certain points during the passage so that difficulties do not develop.

One major job of the temporal legitimator then consists of temporally articulating the passage. Insofar as he does his job, differential temporal expectations do not arise to cause slowdowns or speedups that cause temporal disarray of the sentimental and work orders. The differential temporal expectations held by participants during a given passage follow directly from the type of awareness contexts the legitimator is instituting and maintaining. At certain points or transitions in the passage it may be best to ensure articulation that the passagee and some lesser agents are not aware of the legitimator's more accurate expectations. A closed awareness context helps to keep "things running smoothly." During the last stages of the illness, however, when symptoms raise questions and doubts, an open awareness context — cutting down on differentials in expectations — may keep the passage articulated, because more accurate perceptions are needed to ensure cooperation and coordination of work and sentiment. The patient himself can be part of the work team.[16]

The temporal articulation of a status passage is one aspect, perhaps the major one, of *"generalling" a complex set of multiple passages* — in terms of their multiple directions, timing, motivations and missions, toward an achieving of the mutual, larger goal. Army generals, general engineers, and general contractors are a few types of people who do this kind of work. We shall consider in detail the notion of generalling in Chapter 7 on multiple status passages. In the next chapter we have what could be termed generalling on a very specific and basic issue — how an agent shapes a single passage. We have reserved the term "shaping" for this far less complex theoretical issue. In the largest sense, generalling applies to the articulation of multiple passages, each of which requires shaping so that they will coordinate with the other passages involved in achieving the larger goal or mission of the total project to which they all contribute.[17]

16. Barney G. Glaser and Anselm L. Strauss, *Awareness of Dying* (Chicago: Aldine Publishing Company, 1965) and *Anguish: A Case Study of a Dying Trajectory* (San Francisco: The Sociology Press, 1970).
17. Barney G. Glaser, *The Patsy and the Subcontractor* (in ms.).

4. SHAPING A PASSAGE

THE SHAPE of a status passage is determined by combining its direction and temporality. The term *shape* refers to the line — course of the passage — that results from graphing a status passage when using direction and timing as the two axes. Figure 4.1 gives a hypothetical example of the regularized civil service career. The shape may be any combination of rises, dips (reversals) and plateaus. A basic property of shape is the distance the passagee has traveled in the passage.

Some such picture occurs to those who are attempting to shape a passage. In shaping it they are aware — without actually graphing — whether the passage is moving up, down, or standing still and moving how far over specific periods of time. They bend their efforts accordingly to achieve whatever shape they wish currently and in the future.

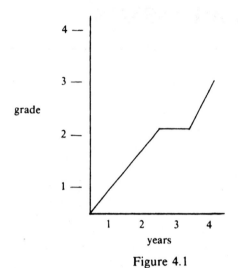

Figure 4.1

Thus, a principle theoretical problem to consider in regard to shaping the passage consists in its control: who is in control and who is vying for control. The control problem varies under three conditions of relevance: shaping a passage as it *exists,* is *discovered,* or is *generated.* Of course, under all three conditions whoever controls must confront the inevitability of continual change as direction proceeds over time. Control is an effort to regulate the changing passage and thus to determine its shape. We shall take up each of the three conditions in turn. Although most of our own work will be on existing passages, much of what we shall say also applies to passages when they are being discovered or generated.

Control of Existing Passages

In this section we shall consider the *means* of control; and in following sections the *balance* of control between agents and passagees; and the handling of passages *out of shape,* which includes various *types of agents and their organization of control.*

MEANS OF CONTROL

One basic way of controlling the shape of a status passage is to prescribe its direction and schedule. Temporal and directional signs ideally are clearly defined and announced. Agents and passagees can expect what the shape of the passage will be with a strong degree of certainty before entering and while they are in it. The certainty of such prescribed passages (which typically occur in large institutions, organizations, or services) enables everyone to recognize both when a passage is out of shape and the manifest reasons for that misshapeness. For example, the high school drop out left because his grades were not good enough to advance to the senior class, leaving his high school passage out of shape. The shapes of such passages are kept at maximum open awareness; and a special defining agent usually is designated to announce formal changes in shape so that all concerned can adjust routinely to whatever prescriptions may be announced.

By contrast, passages with relatively unknown directions and temporal properties are difficult to control with routinized prescriptions. Trouble may easily be created, because routine prescriptions frequently cannot be well fitted to the passage; they generate unfounded notions of delays, lateness, being too fast, and wrong directions. Flexible prescriptions, defined in terms of acceptable limits to shape, can be usefully vested in the hands of control agents who as expert sign readers are ever alert to emerging signs of when and where the passage is going, and why. As these signs are recognized, the agent shapes the passage to within the limits prescribed for a particular transitional stage. This is the job, of course, of doctors or lawyers who have cases whose signs are not always clear. As they read the emergent signs, they try to shape the passage within acceptable moral limits. Thus, doctors will reduce pain, irrespective of narcotic addiction, once sure that a patient will no longer recover from a fatal illness. Before this point occurs, which only he can legitimately determine, morally it is unacceptable to "hook" patients too deeply on narcotics.

Another basic means for controlling the shape of a passage is to prescribe types of persons suitable for it. Thus, to prescribe both the passagees and agents maximizes control over shape during the course of the passage. Getting those agents and passagees requires well organized and conceived processes of recruitment as the basic means for filling the prescriptions. Otherwise the alternative dimensions upon which a passagee or agent are recruited can vary too easily, and later the recruiter may find that the wrong person has been recruited. For example, his chosen liberal candidate is too conservative in office.

Agents may be tempted to take the "wrong" person if they cannot stand the prospect of being a control agent for passage sans passagee. Then the problem becomes not to let the wrong passagee change or destroy the passage or the agent himself.

Prescribed status passages usually exist in organizations and have existing agents formally linked to them, and when agents leave, there are procedures for employing new agents. But *less prescribed, non-institutionalized passages often have no agents until the passagee* (or someone else for him) *recruits one.* Thus, stock market investors must seek a broker. Sick people also are in this position; usually, they must have sufficiently strong physical symptoms to realize illness is in the offing and that they must seek an agent to control it. Some seek these agents to prevent illness; they go for regular check-ups on their teeth or eyes or on their general physical conditions. In these cases, the agents are all around so that a passagee usually chooses his agent according to referrals of other experts, service centers, or friends.

In contrast when passages become generally nonprescribed and noninstitutionalized, then agents may seek passagees and passagees may seek agents — and nothing much happens until they find each other. Then they can create and institutionalize a little pocket of passages so that future mutual searches will not take so long and will be more effective, providing new seekers know about this pocket of institutionalization. Thus, it is still difficult for most potential investors to find a venture investment counselor, and vice versa. But agent and potential passagees both exist, and the best way for them to find each other is to "ask around" in the financial district of a large city. Marginal religious leaders learn how to advertise in the local newspaper for seekers.

A standard way of organizing the recruitment of passagees or agents for a passage is through *comparative selection.* Socially lower-rank selection of passagees and agents is based on broad dimensions of average competence and skill. As one goes up the scale of social rank, recruitment comparisons become based on costs and fees for work and its quality and timing. Comparisons may be socially organized or assumed, such as with the comparative bidding of subcontractors — each submits secret bids through an approved agent, an

1. John Lofland, *Doomsday Cult* (Englewood Cliffs, New Jersey, Prentice Hall, 1966).

organization or a social channel. At the higher socially ranked levels, comparative recruitment is often considered an impropriety, indicating mistrust or crass involvement in costs when the cost should be of minor concern compared to trust and quality. However, lawyers, doctors, stock brokers, accountants, executives, and consultants do not like being compared on criteria such as quality and fees. They wish to be recruited only on trust and given *carte blanche* to guide clients' passages according to their best judgements and with no comparisons made that might subvert their control. Thus, the higher the rank of the agent, the more he wishes this client *not* to have had the controlling fact of comparisons behind his choice of agent.

In some measure, recruiting may entail the *proffering of a passage* to the agent or passagee. A story, ideology, or line about the passage is proffered, and on its basis the person tends either to accept or reject entry to the passage. Proffering is designed to help a candidate discriminate between what is and what is not real about the passage. What is actually proffered, however, may be ideology or myth designed primarily to persuade recruits. Or it may be truth or counter ideology to correct various dimensions of generally known ideology, but this effort still is made to persuade. Mixtures of fact and fiction are usual. Thus the recruit, who does not believe everything, may not know how much and what to believe about the passage. Credibility is lent by official legitimators whose job is to relate authoritatively what the passage will be like, for example, the law office's hiring partner[2] or the firm's personnel manager.

The legitimator's job is to induce the recruit to accept that the passage is as it is presented. Reflection is counseled only on aspects deemed wise by the legitimator, who does not want the recruit to think about aspects that would put the passage out of shape. Too much thought about the passage, especially about moving through it, generally is seen by the agents as potentially annoying or harmful. "Here people just do not think or ask about their next promotion," is the frequent response to potential questions about career. Initial acceptance of the passage leads to recruitment, after which the accepting and rejecting aspects of being an agent or passagee lead to problems that involve continually balancing control and deviance.

2. Erwin O. Smigel, *The Wall Street Lawyer* (New York: The Free Press, 1964), pp. 90-109.

While some undesirable or inevitable passages must have elaborate recruitment procedures by which to force passagees into them (such as imprisonment or the draft), other passages require no recruitment. They just occur; then the passagee must discover that he is in them and exactly where he is in them. This occurs with illness, of course. With the increase of medical control over the shape of chronic illness passages, their shapes are becoming slower and more prolonged, and it is harder to define where one is and how far he will go.

Once in the passage well known, diverse and prevalent means for shaping come to the fore. Agents indoctrinate and train passagees, themselves having been indoctrinated earlier and trained by other agents. Training is accomplished by means ranging from formal programs to informal communication and on-the-job training. Agents and passagees negotiate the shape of a passage as much as they can. Their cooperation is based on acceptable norms and limits, and on deference to others' potentials for control. They juggle others' awareness of the passage through revelation and concealment as a means of insuring that shape evolves in accordance with their own desires. Shape may be controlled under hierarchies of authority that prescribe the delegation of control channels, and prescribe the specific people who will give the orders and the specific instructions that others will obey. Informal groups may exert pressure over agent or passagee, and eventually these may become formally instituted pressure groups.

In studying the shaping of a passage, it becomes important to determine the basic means of its control, which leads to theoretically important questions concerning the balance of control over shaping as each transition comes and goes. Problems of control characteristically will vary with the kind of prevalent means used for control. For example where control is in the hands of one agent who uses an authoritarian control system, problems associated with legitimation of negotiation and with closed awareness contexts will arise easily. An order from above may not be negotiable, as in the army, and passagees often may not be told where they are going and how soon, and thus be unaware of things to come.

BALANCE OF CONTROL

In shaping a passage, a balance of control between agent and passagee tends to be maintained. If this balance is maintained the shaping of the passage is consistent, but if the balance shifts, the shape of the passage is likely to shift.

The classic situation occurs when the *agent holds the balance of power clearly* — at least formally. This situation applies to many client – professional relations. To the best of their ability and judgement, agents shape the passage, and their passagees attempt to exert control generally from a weak position, if at all. When passages attempt control, balance shifts because even the weakest *passagees are not without some resources.*

For example, the following quotation touches on the resources of students, who attempt to use them.

> By practicing the old art of studentmanship, the students in our study managed to exercise some control over the business of becoming a nurse. This was done by deciding what to study for an exam, how to bolster a classmate in the eyes of the faculty, or how best to look enthralled in a classroom or appropriately nursely on a ward. Such concerns, familiar to all students, clearly showed the discrepancy between the reality supported by the faculty and their educational ideology and the reality shaped by the students' common-sense world, between what the school expected from the student and what the student was able and willing to incorporate and project in her emerging professional identity. Further ingredients of the normative structure were compounded by the discrepancy. Legitimate power rested with the faculty and the sole path to becoming a professional was defined by all involved as "getting through nursing school," by learning what the school had to teach. It was the business of the students, given the aspiration to be professional persons, not only to become, but also to convince the faculty that they *were* becoming. Therefore, discrepancies, which by definition imply inability to become, slowness in becoming, or just sheer recalcitrance, had somehow to be softened, diluted and hidden, if not altogether overcome. The arts of studentmanship were paramount here.[3]

Other examples of passagees' partial control are replete in sociology, for instance the restriction of output phenomenon discovered in the Hawthorne studies,[4] or the client control of private medical practice through referral systems.[5] Potential withholding of cooperation as-

3. Virginia Olesen and Elvi Whittaker, *The Silent Dialogue* (San Francisco: Jossey Bass, 1968), p. 150.

4. Elton Mayo, *The Human Problems of an Industrial Civilization* (New York: Viking Press, 1960), pp. 53-74.

5. Eliot Freidson, "Client-Control and Medical Practice," *American Journal of Sociology,* Vol. 65 (January, 1960), pp. 374-382.

sumed to be forthcoming to the person with power remains a tacit control over his not abusing it; this withholding is seen with police and lawyers. In hospitals all levels of staff deliberately react by withholding information from superiors when they wish to punish "uncooperative" supervisors.

Another example is how TB patients may successfully control aspects of their illness career in spite of its domination by public health officials. What the patient cannot do, without ducking out from under the control system entirely, is effectively to shorten the period of chemotherapy. The modal treatment is two years. Indeed, the doctor may deny the patient awareness of a converted sputum to negative — for this announcement legally reduces his power over the patient — so he himself can control the continued treatment. The patient can, however, vary the content of treatment during these two years but cannot often get the period of treatment shortened. A hospitalized TB patient can leave without medical approval; or he can sometimes negotiate for different drugs. Sometimes the TB patient can avoid hospitalization by opting for private care.

A passagee sometimes may wish to avoid completing his passage, because being in passage is far more comfortable or safer than what lies beyond. Thus he tries to shape into his passage a reversal or a slowdown. Universities always have a number of graduate students, who, fearful of graduation, delay completing course work or dissertations. They tend to form "colonies" on or around the campus. Some prisoners and soldiers also colonize institutions, although the prisoners find it more difficult to do so because they must continually break a law to be held or returned to prison; soldiers merely reenlist. Indigent TB patients sabotage their doctor's regimens by not taking medicine in order to stay in the hospital for the shelter and food during the winter. They can also disguise the signs of progress in passage by obtaining negative sputums from fellow patients to submit in places of their own.

Sometimes the issue for the passagee is not one of controlling shape but *how to live while in passage.* Agents may be interested in the matter also, to control the passage. This control may be necessary to the passage (hospitalization of the ill), or it may not be (dormitory requirements for women students or freshmen at a university). In either case, however, the passagee usually will try to exert some control over his style of life while in passage. This is a major issue today for terminal patients in hospitals.[6] Their major effort is to become more informed about their passage so that they can make better demands for living as they wish while dying. When he believes a patient will recover from illness, a doctor can make a patient's style of life more difficult through stringent regimens. However, the life style the passagee wants to control is important to him, but it may not always be important to the agents, if indeed they know what he is doing. For instance, helpless medical faculty have been known to pass highly negative remarks about how marriage cuts in on their students' energies and professional motivations.[7] The faculty may also frown on the "moonlighting" of their residents because it diminishes energy or gives poor professional experience. Faculty can combat the moonlighting sometimes by arranging for "good learning" jobs for their residents. (If they are not in great competition for residents, or do not rely unduly on them for service, they can forbid moonlighting and punish it by ousting the offender.)[8]

When control over style of life is not necessary to the passage, passagees revolt or are simply nonobeisante (as with students in off-campus menages). Usually they continue as long as agents do not yield their "unnecessary" control. Passagees are attempting to make the control specific to the particular passage to free themselves for other activities and passages. The recent rebellion of Catholic priests who wish the right to marry — some even leaving the Church to marry — clearly illustrates this. In such efforts to render general control over specific shape, the juggling of awareness contexts becomes paramount. Styles of living that conflict with the passage are kept clandestine or made very public, depending on the kind of control and change that passagees wish to achieve.

The most extreme resource is for a passagee actually to destroy the passage because he lacks ability to exert a more moderate control over it. For example, in the current rash of student demonstrations,

6. Barney G. Glaser and Anselm L. Strauss, *Time for Dying* (Chicago: Aldine Publishing Company, 1968) and *Anguish* (San Francisco: The Sociology Press, 1970).

7. Howard S. Becker *et al.*, *Boys in White* (Chicago: University of Chicago Press, 1961).

8. Taken from Rue Bucher's study of "socialization."

some students avowedly act to bring down an "establishment" unresponsive to their desires or demands. Another extreme, but more frequently used resource, is to "drop out" of the passage, even when it means giving up a home, marriage, career, or nation. The use of both these extremes is generated when there seems to passagees virtually no means of getting a control agent to change or be changed.

Thus in formal examinations, such as state boards to certify one for entrance to a profession, the candidate may have no notion of who the control agent evaluating the examination is, and the candidate may have no channel to appeal negative decisions. The candidate who does not do well enough to pass may easily feel under this condition that the decision was biased or based on unofficial criteria. Thus, for example, young psychiatrists who fail in achieving entrance to psychoanalytic institutes may in later years find themselves serving on a state psychiatric board's examination committee and are thereby in a position to pass on psychoanalysts taking state board examinations. As control agents with near absolute power, they can easily be accused of seeking retribution when failing a psychoanalyst. The latter may then give up trying for this state of his passage, feeling such arbitrary control is not worth fighting.

The efforts and resources of passagees in weak positions of power *vis-a-vis* control agents give rise to problems of lack of cooperation, recalcitrance, misrepresentation of actions and history, withdrawal, guises to conceal true actions, and destructiveness. The solution to these problems always proposed by well intentioned bystanders, witnesses, and experts is to give passagees more control over their own passage and its destiny and timing. Control agents often do little in this direction except hedge and give lip service to this solution until forced by law, authority, or revolt.

Matters change when levers are built into the agent – passagee relationship to allow the balance of control to shift back and forth. Several basic leverages of control for the passagee are: to "give his business" to the agent or not; to pay his control agent or not; to compare control agents to judge and choose them; to dismiss or fire the agents; to obtain the freedom to think, discuss, and negotiate issues of the passage; not to be personally vulnerable to the necessity of having the service of a control agent, either through not really needing the service or being quickly able to get it from another control agent. Such leverages of control may be easily and expectedly available to the passagee, as when he has to choose a bank or a subcontractor.

In these passages when passagee and agent each can intermittently exert enough control to obtain desired shaping to the passage, characteristically there is a *contest for control* over aspects of direction and timing. For example, in negotiating and accepting bids for a subcontracting job, the homeowner has the power to choose among contractors. After the choice, the subcontractor has the power to control timing of the job and often will not comply with his promised timing but use his power to enforce delays. The homeowner must put up with these delays in the course of the job until power switches back to him. He may get terribly angry — which subcontractors cannot stand — he may cancel the contract, or he may refuse interim payments in order to regain control over the timing. In his turn, the subcontractor may do the job "at last" or give a token performance but still delay, and he can place a lien on the home if he is not paid for the completed job.

The balance of control shifts intermittently as each party resorts to both institutionalized and informal means for influencing the shape of the passage. The important issue to maintaining balance is that neither agent nor passagee relinquishes the controls provided by the nature of the passage. If either does, the other will shape it to his own requirements — which also entail his meeting the temporal responsibilities of his other passages.

Sometimes, although the balance of control is equal enough, passagees fail to use their resources because of more general social values of respect and deference. Brokers, bank officers, and doctors gain a social deference that tends to cede them more control over the passage than they actually should have. While the passagee may have few resources for controlling his doctor he has many normal, obvious ones for controlling his broker or banker. If his deference becomes too binding, he loses a control over his investing or banking that he should ordinarily have to protect himself. We all know of some stock brokers who "churn" the money of investors for commissions under the guise of initiating them into buying and selling. Bankers, however, adjust interest rates and credit in accordance to the demands or the lack of demands by clients. But as the passage proceeds, the passagees are likely through experience to drop the deference that inhibits their measure of control over the passage.

In becoming an investor or banking client, then, the passagee must engage in the contest of control allowed by the balance built into the passage — or take the consequences. *If the passagee does not take some control, the agent will take as much as possible when the delegation of work and authority for the passage is originally worked out.* Later, regaining some control from the agent is more difficult than if one initially assumed it when the grounds for the passage were agreed on.

One strategy a passagee may use in the initial stages is to let the agent spell out the passage in detail. Then he will allocate to himself those aspects of general control over shape that will limit the operations of his agent. The passagee gradually discovers the agent's capacities and uses him only for them. If the agent will not detail the passage, the passagee must probe for it. In effect, the passagee turns the control agent into an operational man who only handles details without general powers. The control agent may be miffed at his loss of general control, but for his part the passagee yields this control at his own peril. If the passagee yields, the chances are increased both for the agent getting what he wishes and for creating an undesirable passage for the passagee. In such passages, agents with the edge in control tend to favor their own fates over the passagees'! Commissions, profits, time, other clients, and comfort are at stake. This is the contest for balance of control that occurs, for example, in dealings with subcontractors, brokers, bankers, lawyers, doctors, and accountants.

The passagee can also limit the control agent's information so that he can control only details rather than the general direction and timing of the passage. The passagee controls the awareness context concerning the passage. Without sufficient knowledge the agent cannot generalize the passage; he focuses only on detailed operations. He lacks a proper context for its appropriate modification because he does not know enough. Thus, brokers, bankers, subcontractors, and accountants are empowered only to accomplish their specific, detailed jobs. If the passagee is naive or too trusting and gives full disclosure of his passage, he will yield enough information to allow general control by such agents. (Accountants with enough knowledge tend to act as business advisers.) Then he may have to stake a claim to general control and put up with the "static" of contrary suggestions and doubts — which the agents give to regain more control for themselves.

The passagee may have to use both of these strategies in some combination — allow or probe for detailing the work, while withholding information — fairly, quickly, and adroitly because during the first round in the contest for balance of control, positions are negotiated quickly. At the first encounter the passagee will have to take as much control as possible. To regain control, thereafter, he may have to switch to new agents. These strategies apply particularly to institutionalized, voluntary passages.

When, in contrast, a passage is innovative, the passagee may find the opposite problem: to get a control agent to accept some control and responsibility. Here the balance is based on some reciprocity of control. If the agent will exert control, the passagee agrees both to comply with it and to exert his share of control. This happens when a student seeks an adviser for a graduate degree dissertation, and the burden is on the student to convince the adviser to sponsor and guide the work.

The strategies apply in reverse when agents wish passagees to take over more control of their passage. The agent will detail as much as possible all the necessary information to make the passagee aware enough to general his own passage and to reduce the agent's work. This happens in chronic illness passages, where doctors try to get the patient to assume control over his own life and treatment regimen. These are long-range passages where as much freedom is desired by the agent as by the passagee. This desire reduces the negative impact of the passage on the life style of the passagee.

The leverages of control a passagee may use also may be claimed and acted upon, even when the agent has disavowed their use as leverages. The leverages then alter the balance of control in those situations, where the control agent has the power to dominate the passage. Thus, while the average client will probably not exert these leverages over a doctor or lawyer, some clients who have enough information, or have been exploited, or have had unsuccesscul experiences with previous experts learn that they actually have more control than they had assumed. They exert this control and start shaping aspects of their passages. They also gain more control over their styles of life while in passage.

The use of these leverages of negotiating details and information is clearly illustrated by the TB patient who goes to a private doctor.[9] Compared to the public patient, he saves money and time through shorter hospitalization at lower rates. He may even avoid hospitalization altogether. He can negotiate his regimen for fewer drugs over a shorter period of time, if his case is not severe. A public patient has less latitude for negotiation and is likely to be hospitalized or on drugs over longer periods of time. The private patient can spend more time discussing his fate and regimen with his doctor, and, with his doctor's trust, manage the regimen at home. Thus, the private patient helps shape his own passage and style of living, while his other passages do not suffer so much. His doctor prevents the public-care system from taking over the passage, if the patient does not abuse his control over the passage. The doctor may use the threat of the public control system to prevent abuse of control by the patient.[10]

This ability of the passagee to exert control is what attracts people to passages linked with private rather than public systems, whether they involve care, training, or financing. But the passagee must still exert his control, or the balance of power will favor the control agent. An example of strong exertion of control is that enforced by parents in private schools in the names of their children. The children complain or suggest improvement so that their parents exert control over the teachers, control based on holding the school's purse strings. Parents of children in public schools do not have the leverage and can act with less effect, except where strong PTA's exist.

Interdependence: An important condition which affects the passagee's and agent's balance of control over a passage is the nature of their interdependence. A primary question is whether either can go on without the other in the passage. If one can, they are *contingently* interdependent; if not, they are *mutually* interdependent. For example, some passagees with special problems or skills are contingently interdependent upon a particular control agent as the only person able

9. Walter Klink, *Problems of Regimen Compliance in Tuberculosis* (Unpublished Ph.D dissertation, Columbia University, 1969).

10. Eliot Friedson, *Patients' View of Medical Practice* (New York: Russell Sage Foundation, 1961).

to help them through either a passage or a transitional phase of it. A slow reader may be very dependent upon a particular teacher who is adept at helping such children. Without this special teacher the child's passage stops. An advanced music student may be contingently dependent upon learning from a master teacher who can coach him to greater heights of perfection. In both cases, the agent is not dependent on the passagee.

The research physician becomes involved in a *mutually* interdependent passage when involved in a research project with a patient passagee — his own research passage may come to a halt or go into reversal depending on the fate of his patient. Partnerships are usually mutually interdependent.

Intersecting interdependence occurs when either agent or passagee can go on with his own passage without the other, or reestablish his passage with another. It is typical of expert-client relations. For example, an ill person decides to treat his own ailment or get a new doctor. Clients can change experts when they are supposedly interchangeable. Couples wishing to build a home can easily go through several architects.

The type of interdependence that exists for a passage will become a major factor in the balance of control over it. Unless other factors mediate, obviously, the balance of control is intermittently equal, both in mutual interdependence and in intersecting interdependence. In the latter, either the agent or the passagee can leave and find an equivalent interchangeable substitute; and in the former type of interdependence both persons need and must compromise with each other. In the contingent passage, however, the person who cannot go on without the other is vulnerable to his control. The passagee must resort to other leverage, and be subtle — using slow downs, delays, threats of quitting — when he wishes to affect the shape of the passage.

In a contingent passage, an effective leverage to be used alone or with other leverages by the dependent person is to keep closed the awareness context relevant to some aspect of the passage. This maneuver affects the shape. Thus, a diabetic child may not tell his mother about eating candy on the way home from school.[11] The awareness

11. Jeanne C. Quint, *Becoming Diabetic: A Study of Emerging Identity* (Unpublished D.N.S. dissertation, Univ. of Calif., San Francisco, School of Nursing, 1969.)

context may not open up until guilt forces the child to tell, or his mother or physician discovers evidence of transgressions. The beautician may not tell a client about a mistake in cutting her hair, hoping she will not discover and report it, thus hurting her career. The beautician covers the mistake by working it into the total configuration of the hairdo.

Because each passage has many aspects of direction and timing, leverage through closed awareness on these aspects is usually ready and temporarily available for affecting its shape. If the dependent person is found out, he must support the sanctions of the control agent to survive the passage. These sanctions are designed to discourage his concealing information again and are aimed at bringing the passage back into a shape desired by the agent or changing it toward better control by the agent. The diabetic child now is questioned thoroughly on arriving home from school: the work of the beautician now is inspected by her boss.

If the control agent becomes so involved in a contingent passage in which the passagee is dependent it turns into a mutually interdependent passage and there is a consequent loss of some of his control. This happens in nursing, particularly in private nursing, when the nurse may become so involved with, say, a dying patient that she must see his life through to the end. Then she loses her power to leave the passage at will, and is more susceptible to the demands of the patient and his family. These demands may counter or modify her controls over the patient's treatment and style of living. She may be more lax about medicine, pain killers, eating, and so forth because she is asked to fudge on the physician's regulations for the patient. However, the private doctor is also, at this point, likely to be mutually involved so will let the laxness pass. Such a contingent passage could also change to mutual with a hospital nurse. The nurse's growing involvement turns the passages to mutual interdependence; this can be broken only by someone's forcing the nurse to quit the case, by the death of the patient, by her own illness, or by being rotated from the ward at the hospital. Thus, contingent interdependence may be stable or likely to change to another type because of the direction and temporal quality of a passage. For a quick death, say a heart attack, a contingent passage is stable; there is no time for mutual involvement to grow.[12]

A residual type of interdependence is the *independent or solo passage,* where the passagee is his own control agent, such as in the careers of solo doctors, lawyers, and consultants. In other fields, people who have not had an education or a specific education can train themselves. Solo passagees tend to feel either very proud at having made it on their own without any help (their solo shaping was successful), or they feel very neglected by not having had a control agent who took an interest in them or who was provided by the "establishment" (their solo shaping left something to be desired).

OUT OF SHAPE: MILD DEVIANCE

Because a passage is in constant motion and shaping is a constant problem involving control, the passage can easily go out of shape. Until this condition is corrected, the passagee or agent experiences perceptions and feelings of *mild deviance* from the projected shape of the passage. For the experience to be more than mild, drastic reversals or blockages must occur, such as an unanticipated demotion in a promising career. Generally, the problem is one of controlling only mild deviances, such as occur from small failures, reversals, speedups, or delays that lead to the passage's getting out of shape for a time. For instance, a doctor may forget to leave an order for pain medication and is unable to be reached for a day, or a lawyer is unable to go to court one day and ruins the current timing of a lawsuit.

Another frequent source of mild deviance derives from an *inability or failure to read the signs of passage, and opportune moments of control are missed.* An illness is left to run its course for quite a while by the sick person who fails to recognize that he is ill until too late for preventing its severity, as in glaucoma. Experts are needed to read signs that are unclear to most non-experts. Experts, who do not fit becoming the agent for the passage, usually refer the passagee to a consulting agent. These referral agents recommend seeing the appropriate type of doctor, lawyer, accountant — usually referring to a particular one who is expert in diagnosing particular conditions. An expert's readings of dire signs may be casual when they are concerned

12. Barney G. Glaser and Anselm L. Strauss, *Awareness of Dying* (Chicago: Aldine Publishing Co., 1965).

with a person for other reasons, but the reading of signs by the consultant may be purposeful when they are sought for an opinion by a passagee or referral agent who feels something is happening but does not know what it is. For instance, at the outset of multiple sclerosis, the patient and his general physician, from casual readings, are led to seek the consultation of a neurologist.

When the signs are clear to the passagee or control agent that the passage is out of shape, it continues because of denying this condition or from involvement in passages elsewhere. In either case, the agent or passagee must use tactics to get the other concerned and to accept his own readings of the passage to correct its shape. Thus, a teacher may have to have a "heart-to-heart" talk with a student who either is denying his impending low grade or devoting his time to other activities at the expense of his course work.

Denying that a passage is out of shape is different from refusing to accept the passage.[13] The denying person, once brought to realize the problem, will help correct its shape. The person who will not accept the passage wants to change either its shape or some aspects of it. One source of not accepting a passage — by passagee or agent — is a dim view of the consequences of accepting and participating in its regular shape. These views easily occur in institutional and organizational contexts where regularized passages abound. The dangers of accepting the standard shape of an organizational career provide a useful example. It may become obvious to a person after his initial transition into the career that anyone who "end runs" the organizational career will move upward faster and better than people who accept the standard directions and timings of the career.[14] The end-runner uses such tactics as soliciting sponsors, engaging in unconventional behavior, and making threats. Sponsors will jump him over others' heads rather than have him wait his turn or replace a superior who is being promoted. This kind of sponsorship puts the careers of other people out of shape — particularly the ones in the standard, prescribed career. The end-runner may succeed beautifully; in the

13. Robert K. Merton, "Social Structure and Anomie," on distinction between innovation and rebellion, in *Social Theory and Social Structure* (New York: The Free Press, 1957), pp. 131-161.
14. Morris Janowitz, *The Professional Soldier* (New York: The Free Press, 1960), pp. 145-48.

meantime accepting persons are locked in for long, uncertain periods of waiting, which, if too long, may kill their abilities to grow. The accepting way becomes the wrong way; concern for order becomes self-defeating. Unconventional behavior causes mild deviance but also causes the noticing of exceptional skills that are needed in executive positions.[15] Developing job contracts elsewhere, even moonlighting to receive offers of another job, also threatens the current organization into moving the person along faster to keep him in the organization. The end-runner is alert to using any device and many devices in combination as he discovers their potentialities.

The clever end-runner tries his best to conceal his tactics. He maintains a closed awareness context with respect to them. To see another person moving faster through some deviant actions hurts the morale of others in the passage who have accepted and trusted its prescribed shape. Then, if all start not accepting and begin to end-run, the passage itself may be destroyed or changed drastically. The result for the end-runner — who is basically committed to the passage sufficiently to want only specific changes for himself to achieve more faster in the same career — is either to have no recognizable passage or to be severely reprimanded in order that the passage be saved. His mild deviance then becomes severe, with severe consequences. He keeps, therefore, the awareness context as closed as possible until he gets his promotion, which as a *fait accompli* opens the awareness context, but too late for creating much disorder or instability. What changes might occur will be quickly handled to put the passage back in shape. Other passagees then reap the innovative benefits to shape derived from the tactics of the end-runner, who is now safely ahead of them. The control agents have preserved the passage. Regularization of the innovation, however, may render them powerless to quicken subsequently the pace of other passagees, when the changes originally were effective only for one person without competition. An unconventional display of skill becomes a conventional process so that the competition becomes keener. The end-runner may have looked good enough only in a situation where there was no competition!

Another source of nonacceptance is that the passage itself is discovered by the passagee as "not designed for people like him." He

15. Barney G. Glaser (Ed.) *Organizational Careers* (Chicago: Aldine Publishing Company, 1968), "Sources and Strategies of Promotions," pp. 191-259.

may discover and create better alternatives within an organization or elsewhere. He may not like the context of the passage; he may not like the growing responsibility to an organization that limits his freedom; he may wish more control over his fate; he may learn to doubt or suspect the manifest intent of control agents. In trying to train a passagee, an agent may try to hook him, as when engineers are coached into administration and out of "bench work" with opportunity, rank, money, or when an insurance agent instructs a client on the liability dangers all around him.[16]

To reshape the passage, an unaccepting passagee may be removed because his mild deviances are uncorrectable; the student who never gets to class on time or who constantly misses his exams is dropped. Control agents may redefine the passage or its purpose for the passagee to instill new meaning or spend time coaching the extant meaning back into the passagee. For example, a parent or teacher tries to get a dropout back into school. They give the proverbial "talking to" before taking stronger measures to nip deviance in the bud. The fear of more severe reprimands, if corrections are not made, may bring the passagee back in line. Sometimes a removal or correction of a passagee requires a form of degradation ceremony; its impact is to restore the passage to shape for remaining passagees.[17] They view the negative sanctions as support for current shaping: one sticks with the regular shape to avoid the penalties visible even for mild deviance. The soldier's compliant passage through training — especially with examples of punished deviance in clear view — is an example.

Over-accepting of a passagee or agent can also put the passage out of shape. Over-accepting may come from indoctrination or idolization, or from a rigid need to confrom to requirements, or from strong institutional emphases on what is important. The passage gets out of shape because the over-accepting person tends to blur or prevent discriminations that ordinarily keep someone sensitive to all factors involved. (A vivid example was the excessively rigid officer in the *Bridge on the River Kwai.*) Over-accepting of a prominent factor leads to neglect of other factors, hence the passage may go awry. Students

16. Simon Marcson, *The Scientist in American Industry* (New York: Harper & Row, 1960), pp. 61-70.
17. Harold Garfinkel, "Conditions of Successful Degradation Ceremonies," *American Journal of Sociology* (1956) 61, 420-24.

who are too intent on getting good grades because of institutional emphasis may develop techniques which mitigate against learning.[18] Scientists who are too intent on obtaining recognition may "juggle" their research to achieve it.[19] Well-indoctrinated psychiatrists, without the ballast of other theory or knowledge, may do more harm than good to sensitive patients, who are taught by them to think themselves ill according to psychiatric theory.

Sociologists, who take the everyday rhetoric and assumptions of social mobility that "sound right" and proceed to study them, actually study what is not going on. They engage in what may be termed "good citizens' research," while social problems that follow from the realities of social mobility go unscrutinized.[20] Eventually, the negative feedback, say from a colleague or from Black Power advocates, may put a sociologist's career in this area out of shape. He realizes he must start new studies that involve questioning long accepted assumptions of opportunity and ways of rising and falling in American society. He must study mobility conditions and the assumptions supporting them and not assume either.

In short, keeping a passage in shape requires that the agents and passagees constantly balance their degrees of acceptance so as not to reject or accept too much at the expense of changes that require new assumptions. Changes in various aspects and constant motion over time are the two elements of the passage that make accepting it a process rather than a static *fait accompli.* No matter how scheduled and prescribed the passage, acceptance as process leads the passagee and agent to be ever alert to emerging changes that may modify its direction and temporality. For the noninstitutionalized passage, acceptance is clearly a process of emergence, because direction and temporality vary as the passage progresses and the parties to it make the appropriate discoveries.

Another prominent source of a passage going out of shape is *an incompetent or inappropriate agent.* Going to the wrong or incompetent specialist can put a patient's illness career out of shape. When the

18. Howard S. Becker and Blanche Geer, *Making the Grade* (New York: John Wiley & Sons, Inc., 1968).

19. Robert K. Merton, "Priorities in Scientific Discovery: A Chapter in the Sociology of Science," *American Sociology Review,* XXII (Dec., 1957), pp. 635-59.

20. Anselm Strauss, *The Contexts of Social Mobility* (Chicago: Aldine Publishing Company, 1970).

passage cannot be put back into shape — irreversible harm or unto-ward discomfort is done to the patient — malpractice suits are liable to result.

An inappropriate agent may operate within either a closed or open awareness context. If he chooses the latter context, he will explain to the passagee that the passage is not "my type" and suggest that the client go elsewhere. This is, of course, a frequent occurrence in service occupations where there is referral of customers to the appropriate specialist. If the agent who does not fit the passage is not linked to a referral network or does not know in fact who the right kind of agent is, a search for the right control agent will begin. If the passagee is already in passage and helpless, the presumed control agent may feel the moral responsibility to find the correct agent. For example, a policeman will call a doctor if a person is hurt in a street accident. In another example, a local LSD coach was brought a woman who appeared to be on a trip and needing help. The coach soon decided she actually might be suffering from a psychotic break, and started searching for a psychiatrist to help her — but one who would not put her on a 72-hour hold within the county hospital. In the first example the policeman may not know the actual doctor of the accident victim; he just calls an available one. In the second instance, the coach asked around about the kind of psychiatrist who might be appropriate; in the end he called the police and asked them to decide, and they turned her over to the county hospital for observa-tion to determine who was the appropriate control agent to call.

When the passagee is not helpless and is aware, then either he or both he and the inappropriate control agent together may search for a proper agent to put the passage in shape. In searching, they may discover errors in judging what kind of passage they actually have and need an agent for and thereby shape the passage anyway. Often the passagee must go it alone after the inappropriate agent has tried to help somewhat. Then he becomes a "seeker" for an agent who will define and control his passage. People who need some kind of mar-ginal religion or salvation are in this situation.[21]

An inappropriate agent who wishes to operate illegitimately may choose to operate under a closed awareness to keep his true identity

21. Lofland, *Doomsday Cult, op. cit.*

secret as long as possible. Thus a con man is not discovered by the mark until the promised deal does not work out, and perhaps not even then.[22] If the passagee discovers his mistake in working with the wrong agent, he must quit the passage or go it alone or find a legitimate agent to patch up the passage. For illness careers, persons who survive a quack's ministrations will probably go to a doctor for help. Sometimes, even when the passage gets drastically out of shape, the passagee may not admit he went to a wrong or illegitimate agent. Clients adamantly may defend their con men or quack doctors to prove their choice was correct.[23] As an aid to their defense, such a client listens to the agent's justifying explanations about why things are going wrong or are not getting better and believes promises that matters will improve.

If an appropriate agent takes over, he has several options for getting some shape back into the passage. First, he can semilegitimize and then guide the wrong agent. This can be done, providing the latter still has a viable relationship with the passagee, when the legitimacy and shaping derives from a higher authority. Doctors can advise by phone a family member, fireman, policeman, or nurse on how to tend an illness until he gets there, thus putting some semblance of shape back into the illness. If the doctor and, say, the nurse on the scene are at cross purposes, the ensuing shape will be a resultant of their desires regarding timing and direction. When the legitimate agent finally arrives on the scene then he must make a calcualted decision as to how further to resolve the passage. He may ask the semilegitimate agent to leave, considering him worthless, or continue to use him for his close relationship with the passagee but give him no discretionary power. Sometimes he must get rid of the wrong agent who otherwise continues to exert a bad influence.

An inappropriate agent in charge simultaneously may be trying to get himself legitimated while he is putting the passage out of shape! This happens in on-the-job training when barber, dental, or nursing students are doing the job of the professional. While their competence

22. Edwin Sutherland, *The Professional Thief* (Chicago: University of Chicago Press, 1937).

23. Erving Goffman, "On Cooling the Mark Out: Some Aspects of Adaptation to Failure," in Arnold M. Rose (Ed.), *Human Behavior and Social Processes* (Boston: Houghton Mifflin Co., 1962), pp. 482-506.

is not yet complete, they are hoping to prove themselves by controlling (however ineptly) the passage of a client as if they already were full-fledged professionals.[24] Such a student learns from his mistakes, while the client may have to seek repairs or solace from another more adequate agent. In this situation, however, the as yet "inappropriate" control agent may willingly indicate to other agents and perhaps to passagees that he still is not ready to be totally in charge of this passage, if too uncertain of his competence yet and if its admission does not harm his career. This open awareness context is his defense against blame for errors — no subterfuge exists.

This last source of being the wrong agent — a person in training and not yet legitimated — brings out an important distinction that pertains to the shaping of a passage. What might appear to the passagee as deviance in his passage may be, as in the case of a student practice, simply an appropriate transition in his training toward becoming a legitimated agent. This same phenomenon may also occur in the passagee's passage; that is, the deviation actually may be a stage in his passage of which he or others are not aware; therefore, they perceive it as a deviation. For instance, being a hippie for many young men or women may be just another form of "sowing oats" in which young adults engage during their passages toward "responsible" adulthood. Despite what their elders say, their passages may not be out of shape but only be in a new form of the expected shape. Those who criticize any deviation from a passage, therefore, must be sure it is actual rather than only apparent.

Criticism (and its associated abrasive and repressive actions) are the primary controls used to keep a passagee in line and his passage in shape. Many people in training passages will court such criticism from agents to keep themselves in line and to keep learning. But criticism used for *apparent deviance,* when the passage is not really out of shape but in a difficult transition, may cause actual deviance. The passagee may rebel and repudiate the control agent; he may become defensive toward what he feels are unfounded controls; he may become the deviant he is expected to be. This potential for creating true deviance puts a premium on a control agent's knowing

24. Blanche Geer *et al.,* "Learning the Ropes, Situational Learning in Four Occupational Training Programs" in E. Deutscher (Ed.), *Among the Poor* (New York: Basic Books, 1968), pp. 209-235.

the signs and the transitional statuses of given passage and the ability to catch changes in them so that he can adjust his control accordingly.

Unfortunately, many control agents in this situation make mistakes (parents account for them by the notion of "generation gap"), so mediating agents help to blunt the effect of strong and unfounded criticism before the passage becomes too drastically out of shape. Examples of these agents would be psychiatrists, psychologists, social workers, marriage counselors, parents, good friends, and so forth. For a limited time they are allowed to talk, counsel, control, and negotiate with the control agent and passagee until the latter believes them to have the passage back in shape. The mediator tries to make the various parties recognize their inaccurate perceptions, gets them to compromise and to accept new forms or stages and to begin working together sensibly.

Awareness is an important condition affecting reactions to a passage that is out of shape. If a passagee or a control agent "skips out" on the passage, obviously it becomes out of shape to many others. Awareness of "out of shapedness" comes instantly with the knowledge of skipping, and immediate controls are used to correct the passage. When soldiers go AWOL, patients go A.M.A., prisoners break out, parolees skip town, executives abscond, dragnets are set to catch the person if indeed that is required to put the passage back into shape. If the particular man is not needed, then a replacement is sought through recruitment procedures, the potential replacement being screened for his ability to put the passage back into shape, although perhaps with appropriate changes in direction and timing. Our newspapers are filled with this kind of event which occurs conspicuously in political life: people resign for higher or other jobs or when they believe their political usefulness is over and new candidates are proposed.

When the deviance of a control agent or passagee is concealed, wittingly or unwittingly, then the passage may not be discovered as out of shape for some time — and perhaps only when it is too late to reshape it. The con man may keep the mark's losses and liabilities concealed from him until the timing of the passage literally forces disclosure of its being out-of-shape.[25] In the dying passage this hap-

25. Goffman, *op. cit.*

pens also when the course of illness forces awareness that recovery will not occur.[26] In both cases the passagee must accept the deviances. As a resolution, the con man will cool the mark down and out of the passage. The doctor will redefine the patient's passage so that as it proceeds it will again expectedly be in shape, however undesirable.

Passagees also may conceal deviances that eventually put the passage out of shape. The TB patient who flushes his pills down the toilet will eventually be discovered when he does not improve as expected, and indeed may suffer a reactivation (a reversal in direction).[27] This concealment by a passagee of deviating actions usually occurs because he does not wish to undergo undesirable aspects of the passage. Concealment is attempted even at the expense of retarding or blocking or reversing the passage. After the discovery, a control agent becomes more stringent: he makes more frequent and closer surveillance of the passagee. He may return the passagee to a custodial institution or confine him to his home. He may refrain from giving an anticipated early release of the passagee from passage which includes restraint or incarceration, because he does not trust the person to control the end of the passage himself — as he would a passagee who had demonstrated a desire and responsibility to keep his passage in shape.

Those agents or passagees who refuse to go along with the passage put into question by their actions the controls and the desirability — on balance — of the passage itself to other people and organizations and to other agents and passagees. Thus, *to bring the passage back into shape — reaffirm its legitimacy — may require the controls and pressures of persons who are not directly involved.* These others may have indirect delegated responsibility or moral responsibility for seeing that the passage ultimately fits the social necessities of the community. Thus, even mild deviance may have far reaching repercussions. The arbitrary manner in which a policeman may give traffic tickets, the large fees charged by doctors or lawyers that cause patients to avoid them, excessive interest rates or commissions that hold back potential investors — all may spark controls from social, legal, and governmental sources external to the passage. Therefore, agents try to control their colleagues before local governments, administra-

26. Glaser and Strauss, *Awareness.*
27. Walter Klink, *op. cit.*

tions, and communities decide that they must act to control improprieties, because the agents ordinarily in control allow too much deviance in the passages over which they should maintain a proprietous shape.

Discovering a Status Passage

There are many status passages of whose existance passagees are unaware. The control agents involved also may not quite realize the passage exists; they only do what is necessary at appropriate times. Of if they know about the passage, they do not really tell about it because the passage as such is not pushed. Rather it is only revealed to the passagee as he goes along. Thus, he has to discover the passage — its shaping — for himself, sometimes quite without the help of others. Examples of such passages are: becoming an investor, a borrower, a client, or a professional; becoming ill (many illness passages are highly codified); becoming engaged and married in America; becoming a sponsoree (not the career itself); going through pregnancy and childbirth; going through menopause; and becoming a user of drugs.

Discovering pertains to learning and knowing the elements of a "known" passage. Even if one is known by label only, its nature must be discovered by the passagee, as illustrated by a first pregnancy. The pregnant woman, not knowing much about the passage, depends upon the doctor to explain it at strategic points. Discovering pertains also to the passagee's discovery that he is already in a passage he did not know about. This occurs in "becoming" passages such as becoming a marijuana user,[28] and investor or borrower.[29] The passagee only discovers he is in passage after it grows on him, after he is deeply involved and his relationship with a control agent is firm and continuous.

Information or knowledge of a passage allows control over its shape. Therefore when the passagee first begins to discover a passage, he is usually unable to exert effective balancing controls until enough

28. Howard S. Becker, "Becoming a Marijuana User," in Becker (Ed.) *Outsiders,* (New York: The Free Press, 1963).

29. David J. Crabtree and Barney G. Glaser, *Second Deeds of Trust* (Mill Valley, Calif., Balboa Publishing Co., 1969).

of the passage is revealed to him. Considering the time it takes for discovery, the control agent may easily be able to shape the passage to his own conceptions so that the passagee later finds it is difficult to make significant changes. Hence, an agent may prefer passagees who know little and whose passages are only slowly discovered by them. Accordingly, the agent then says as little as possbile, his rationale being that he will say things only as the passagee is ready to understand them at appropriate phases of his passage. It may take years for a new borrower to get the amount of information out of a bank officer, which he could relate in an hour if he so wished. By the time a borrower of money discovers what he has actually "gone through," usually, or at least after, he is hooked on loans and has paid out much more money than was necessary. In these kinds of passages, control agents generally keep the awareness context closed as long as possible.

For passagees who are aware of the undesirable consequences of this structural condition *(no initial control over shaping),* many strategies are available for quickly discovering the passage so that influence on shape can be exerted. The passagee can intensively interview his agent, probing all statements to force information about the passage. He can seek the "one" agent who likes to talk and "square" with clients. The passagee can fake understanding to keep the topic open with the agent. Because agents in this position tend to give specific answers to specific problems to gain immediate closure, thus not revealing too much out of politeness, the passagee can counter by interviewing several agents and then compare their renditions, discovering gaps in accuracy and gaining more information than any one agent may actually have. In this way, especially if he learns a great deal, a passagee can gain considerable control over the initial shaping of his passage. This tactic is formally built into an activity which is based on comparative bidding — subcontracting. The tactic may also be used in obtaining credit or medical and legal help, providing the client has and takes the time to interview and compare potential agents and is not misled by norms against comparisons. The passagee may even learn enough to become his own agent on a do-it-yourself basis, as do many patients and home remodelers.

The passagee must have a relationship to a system to use the information or he must be prepared to act as his own agent in the passage. If the customary control agents will not take on a knowledgeable passagee ("he knows too much") he may have to bootleg his knowledge to obtain a passage. Undercover agents, for example, become assimilated into criminal, drug, marginal, or political groups as naive passagees. In all training passages, it behooves passagees not to act as if they know too much at the beginning. Agents, when they are training people, usually do not wish to deindoctrinate simultaneously, unless in fact they are set up specifically to convert their trainees, as in religious sects.

Sometimes a passagee and an agent must discover the passage together. This occurs with existing passages, as when a new teacher and a new student embark on a standard teaching program that includes discovering as they go along what others already know. What also can occur is that *agent and passagee together actually generate new aspects of passage as they retread and discover an existing passage.*

Generating a Status Passage

The generation of a passage occurs basically in at least two ways. A group of people sit down and figure one out — the *chartered* passage; a passagee with or without an agent generates a passage as he or they go through it, shaping it as they go along — the *emergent* passage. In both cases, uppermost in the minds of participants is control over direction and timing — shape.

The emergent passage is an open-ended, innovative one. In figuring out the passage that is occuring, both passagee and agent are discovering each other's and their own capacities for controlling the shape of the passage — as they decide on its shape. They build a relationship with some degree of reciprocity regarding what they do for each other and what they gain from the passage. They selectively discount as they gather and appraise the facts of what is happening and negotiate a balance of control over what is happening. They may borrow from similar older passages as they discover new ways of acting. If made public, their transactions and innovations may be followed by other people. Examples of emergent passages — perforce now appearing as existant to us — do not abound.

One example involves the venture-investment counselor and the tax-wise investor. Their new passage is now only sufficiently codified within a few offices of major urban financial districts. In this new passage, the stakes are high and the risks great, but the losses are nil because of tax benefits. Problems arise that concern matters such as general *vs.* limited liability and general *vs.* limited responsibility, long *vs.* short terms, the return of capital, tax expertise, corporate forms *vs.* partnership forms. Generally, this passage has been worked out in a general-limited partnership format, wherein the investment counselor or producer takes both control and a larger portion of the profits because of his general liability and greater expenditure of time. After taxes are due and the venture's profit comes in, all parties incorporate and take further capital gains and also look about for a merger with a larger corporation.

Another example is the corporate conglomerate passage that has only become widespread in the last five years. Also, investment clubs — say of women — now are emerging. The LSD trip — involving both coach and tripee — also is a recent emergent passage, as is the hippie marriage (which is different from common-law and licensed marriages). Once these passages are sufficiently worked out, continuing the open-ended, innovative aspects becomes too time consuming, and they are unsupported by the sentimental order. Then people are expected to adhere to the routinized prescriptions of passage.

The chartered passage is set up by the duly authorized people of an organization, group or institution. Their focus, typically, is on providing a career for new clients, employees, or for training students, or for their organization or group. As agents, they themselves may become the future control agents of the passage. The first people to become the agents and passagees are charter members, who will put the passage into effect; they take it "off the books" and carry it out. Many a new passage may remain for months or years on the books before it gets actualized. We are all familiar with grants for training programs that are set up months before staff and students are recruited.

As the agents begin to discuss the shape of the passage — its direction and timing — almost immediately they consider control as a property of each aspect of the passage. Thereby they work out a balance of control that is suited to maintaining the desired shape of the passage they anticipate. If they are potentially among the control agents, they will especially be concerned with their decisions. For example, in starting a new department and developing the student passage, the faculty must decide on the degree of autonomy which a student initially may have to shape his own passage, and they must plan on balancing the control accordingly. In some respects they may wish complete control for certain required basic courses; in others they may wish to give the student autonomy — as with electives, papers, and theses.

In this kind of passage, several other factors impinge on the development of control and shape. If the passage is similar to one which agents have been through themselves, this specific experience is important. In various degrees they will want built into the new passage a recapitulation of the "bright" and correction of the "dull" aspects of their own passages. If these agents came through diverse passages and from different backgrounds, then they will have diverse references; those who liked their previous passage may wish the new passage imbued with traditional timing and directions while those who experienced great previous dissatisfaction may wish their own later stages to be made into the beginning stages of the new passage so passagees will not waste time as they did. If they had no specific experience in the new area, their reference will be too general about such broad types of passage, for instance, how students in general should be trained.

The degree and specificity of experience also are sources for their imagery in the ensuing debate about what the passage should look like and how far and fast it should go. People with specific experience will give brief reviews of their own passages to buttress its suggested repeatability or non-repeatability, and they will feel deeply about what they are saying. Those who base their positions on general knowledge will refer to general values which support their views: their deep feelings rest on these values rather than on specific experiences.

Control over the generated passage will be screened in terms of its implication for the organizational context. People who are likely to be affected will be asked to approve or correct aspects of the planned passage. If others in power do not wish this passage as designed, they refuse to ratify it or modify it greatly. As a result, the charter agents in charge of generating the passage may — as offended people — strike, protest, or actually leave the organization. A current example is the push by black college students for programs in black studies.

Control over the passage will also be influenced by the potential legacy it leaves for the future. The style of the passage, its controls and shape must stand the test of time. Future generations must not be hamstrung too much when attempting to modify the passage to meet new conditions some years hence.

In concluding this and the previous two chapters we must underline that we have only touched on the topics of direction, time and the controlling of shape. We have merely reviewed some problems and categories; there will have been many more connections of theoretical importance that readers have thought of or were spurred on to think about. These chapters were designed to open up and formulate the topics sufficiently so that other social scientists might profitably develop these and similar topics when analyzing their own data.

5. DESIRABILITY

THE DESIRABILITY of a status passage provides the motivational basis for actions that shape the passage. Its shaping results, in part, from the degree of desirability felt by agent and passagee toward the specific dimensions of direction and timing as they unfold. *Desirability pertains both to the passage as a whole and to specific dimensions of it.*

The degree of desirability is also subject to change. For example, while a pregnancy may be considered desirable as a whole, progressively it can become more undesirable for the mother on several specific dimensions. She develops nausea; she becomes increasingly awkward in her movements; her backache increases; her sex life diminishes; and as birth nears she becomes more and more anxious about the delivery and about the potential physical condition of her child.

The strategic question about the desirability of a passage is *"from whose viewpoint the passage is desirable or undesirable"* — with further probing about the dimensions of desirability and the points where desirability or undesirability might progressively change into each other. In this chapter we shall consider the viewpoint of the passagee and his control agents, especially those with stakes in a passage that make it more or less desirable to them. *Stakes* are a principal source for making the passage's desirability a prolonged concern. Stakes in a passage are quite different from the more casual appraisals of desirability that are based on general values, or morality, or the generosity and goodwill held either by people who are uninvolved or by people who are involved but who have no stakes in the passage. Those with vested interests realize that because they desire to participate in or depart from the passage, they must take the consequences of their desired actions.

First we shall consider what happens when both the passagee and the agent view the passage as desirable, *then* when only the agent sees the passage as desirable while the passagee sees it as undesirable. *Next* we shall consider when the agent views it as undesirable while the passagee views it as desirable. *Finally,* we shall consider what happens when both view the passage as undesirable.

The Mutually Desirable Passage

When both the passagee and the agent find the passage desirable, cooperation is its dominant characteristic. Both work together to achieve a desirable passage. Differences that might cause conflicts or recalcitrance refer to minor dimensions of the passage, otherwise it would be held sufficiently undesirable by one or both parties. For example, cooperation colored with minor conflicts and slight recalcitrance certainly is typical of the student passage toward a professional degree, of other training passages, and of sickness passages when there are expectations of good recovery.

In working together to achieve a desirable passage, the passagee and the agent may develop differences over what they find desirable.[2] One difference is over whether to complete or prolong the passage. Either may find it desirable *only* as a passage in action,

1. For a series of articles on the cooperative bases of mutually desirable passages see, Barney G. Glaser (Ed.) *Organizational Careers* (Chicago: Aldine Publishing Company, 1968), "Part II, Recruitment to Organizational Careers," pp. 55-111. These articles include Simon Marcson, "The Recruitment of Industrial Scientists;" David Reisman, "Recruitment to the Academic Career;" Erwin O. Smigel, "Recruitment of Wall Street Lawyers;" David Sills, "Recruiting Volunteers;" and Theodore Caplow and Reece McGee, "Procedures of Academic Recruitment."

2. William Kornhauser, "Professional Incentives in Industry," in his *Scientists in Industry* (Berkely: University of California Press, 1962), pp. 117-56.

therefore not wish it to end. He wants to make an entire life of his passage, keeping it going as long as possible. At the same time, the other person may be striving for closure. Sometimes prolonging is a worthy end, as in a long-range organizational career (military or government) or in a chronic illness with probable death at the end (diabetes). At other times, this aim can block either growth or the undertaking of a new passage that might begin after the current one ends. In the latter case, the passagee may have to slow down the passage, even reverse it at times, to prevent normal closure from occurring. Thus, we have the perpetual graduate student and the perpetual child both unwilling to take on the responsibilities and autonomy of the next passage. We also have as instances those agents who keep the passagee dependent and perpetually in passage — some mothers, doctors, and sponsors. Desirability can be a force for completing or prolonging the passage. When the passagee and agent diverge on this or other central dimensions of desirability their cooperation is easily subverted. If cooperation breaks down completely, there exists a condition wherein either one sees the passage as undesirable — as it is turning out. Then conflict and recalcitrance become characteristic accompaniments of the passage.

CEREMONIES

When closure is completely desirable to both passagee and agent, *ceremonies* that mark transitions and the end may occur, heralding the desirability of passage. A ceremony buttresses the sentimental order of a passage as one that actually achieves desirable ends. These ceremonies are especially important when the passage itself is not too desirable, but the achieved goal is. The ceremony then symbolizes having travelled a rough path to success, for example, that travelled in professional schools that have courses amounting to "survival training."

The ceremony also can symbolize forced endings for passages so desirable that prolonging can only be terminated by formal acknowledgement, or the participants might never quit — such as a graduation that forces a youth to leave college ("the best years of his life") and go to work. Because these formal ceremonies are scheduled, they temporally and clearly shape the passage for those who wish to prolong it, as well as for those who wish to end it. The ceremonies also are given formal announcement far in advance so that people may have definite temporal expectations; thus they can savor the passage while it lasts — anticipate the rewards of closure and of terminal honors.

Ceremonial endings maximize the open awareness context around the successfully completed desirable passage. Lists of young lawyers passing the bar are published. Young fathers pass out cigars, and mothers send out birth announcements. Others, who are not involved in the passage, send congratulations acknowledging the desirability of the passage and its happy ending. In contrast, the ending of an undesirable passage may be responded to either with condolences, if the ending is unhappy, or congratulations if it means being rid of an unhappy passage. However, the ending of desirable passages can be unhappy when it appears that there is no longer any desirable action either for the agent or the passagee — as in retirement or after being fired, or after working for an organization that has been dissolved. Then, condolences can be offered by others. But congratulations are offered to the man who has planned another new desirable passage for himself. He is applauded by others for continuing to base his life on a new and desirable passage, which is of central concern to himself or his family. In short, people find it desirable to have their fellows involved in desirable passages as central organizing features to their lives.

SOCIAL INTEGRATION

The degree of desirability of a status passage depends both on the degree to which a man is socially integrated into groups and on the social circumstances that provide such desirable passages. For example, in so far as someone is integrated into an occupation that is amply rewarded, chances are he will have a desirable work passage. Or if a man belongs to social groups or lives in social circumstances that support, say, stable marriage relationships, he is likely to have either a desirable marital life or leave one that does not measure up. Divorce — terminating the undesirable — is in the service of finding a mutually desirable passage with a new partner.

As social integration turns to social isolation, and central desirable passages supported by circumstances and groups are harder to find or achieve, another type of desirable passage emerges. By and large, it is a *socially alienated passage with only apparent mutual desirability* for both agent and passagee alike.[3] It tempts both, who during its initial transitions, are delighted with the passage and unmoved by, or do not think about, its potentially undesirable ending. In their isolation they focus on prolonging the desirable passage, unmindful that it constitutes a way of escaping from participating in socially integrated and desirable passages.

Examples abound: women take up prostitution, young people take up criminal pursuits, drugs, drifting, ganging, and so forth. The passage is entered voluntarily because its temptations are great. Initially the successes of the passage may bring forms of satisfaction, (money, sex, companionship, love, "trips"); these further seduce the passagees and their agents so that they continue with the passage. But the shape of such desirable passages includes inherent reversals that are forced by the social context in which the passages occur. The prostitute literally wears out and is less in demand; the pimp, criminal, and the drug addict or user are busted too often and so put out of circulation. Representatives of the city or state may put the passagees and the central agents of these apparently desirable passages into the undesirables — making them institutional inmates or perhaps coupling prison with a rehabilitation dimension (which some consider desirable even if duller than aspects of their freer existences).

The temptation of apparently desirable passages is reinforced by the social isolation of passagee and agents, which leaves them with little else to do or avenues to pursue, both in terms of structural opportunities and awareness of alternatives.[4] Further, their isolation may even make them unaware of the undesirable consequences that lie ahead. Even if they are dimly aware, surely their isolation helps them deny undesirable future consequences because initial pleasures dominate their lives, and confrontations with negative consequences are still limited. They maintain their isolation as long as possible during the passage, while other people who dwell on negative aspects

3. Epy Chinoy, *Automobile Workers and The American Dream* (New York: Random House, 1955), see "The Chronology of Aspirations of Automobile Workers," pp. 110-22.

4. Edwin Sutherland, *The Professional Thief* (Chicago: University of Chicago Press, 1937) and W. I. Thomas, *The Unadjusted Girl* (New York: Harper & Row, 1967).

of the passage tend further to isolate and reject them. The passage itself may become one of intense involvement and investment if the stakes are high. Isolation is broken through only when reversals start to occur, unwanted consequences begin to appear, and the passage begins to break down and is wiped out by physical incarceration or personal destitution as the agents of social integration block the passage.

NEGOTIATION

When a passage is mutually desirable both to agent and passagee, their cooperation may focus on negotiating mutually acceptable terms of the passage. [5] For each, the passage is more or less desirable, as based on the terms and stakes involved. Negotiations occur around the best terms (money, time, procedures, division of labor, etc.) possible for each and continued mutual desirability to both. Negotiations are based on initial stakes in the passage and their increase or decrease as derived from the original terms of passage. Examples include negotiating for a career in an organization, negotiating for a job with an architect, and negotiating during the annual collective bargaining.

The desirability of the passage to all parties steers the balance of power involved in the negotiation toward compromise to preserve the passage. Conflicts that might dissolve the passage are avoided. If the balance of power tips excessively in either direction, the stronger party will not really prevail because imbalance will destroy the mutually desirable passage. Thus, the weaker participant gains equity in power from the desirability of a passage; otherwise he might easily be over-dominated or controlled or even wiped out. The person with excessive power has too much at stake in the relationship to wipe out or dominate the weaker one. Thus, students are not failed in courses when they might be but are coached in areas in which they are weak; poor credit risks are given time or even new loans to help them make up delinquent payments.

The power that the weaker participant gains because of mutual desirability of the passage is, however, a *"false" power.* Should the passage become undesirable to the stronger party for some unforeseen

5. Glaser, *op. cit.,* section on "Motivations Within the Organization," pp. 111-161. Articles include Morris Janowitz, "Military Career Motivations," Simon Marcson, "Career Development of Scientists," and Harold L. Wilensky, "Careerist Types."

change in circumstances, the weaker one may be completely subjected or wiped out. The weaker, then, must endeavor either to keep the passage desirable for the stronger in some fashion as, say, one spouse may keep a marriage going at all costs, however personally undesirable, or submit to its dissolution.

Negotiating can be continual, ever changing, to mirror changes in the shape and stakes of a passage. Such *continual negotiating* is, however, less usual than *scheduled negotiation.* The former puts both passagee and agent under continual strain of revamping their compromises, as stakes shift, to prevent the passage's dissolution through mistakes or surprise swings in its shape. It is hard to find examples of continually negotiated passages because such a strain is imposed on it, not by the participants, who always wish to avoid strain, but by the nature of the passage itself, which will not be ordered or shaped sufficiently long enough to warrant compromises that endure. For many years travel over land, sea, and air was of this nature: captains were continually negotiating the passage with crews, leaders with travelers, as unforeseen weather, geographical, and social conditions constantly changed the passage. Now, with weather reports, planned itineraries, flight plans, surrounding controls of foreign population, and so forth, such passages can be negotiated in advance to ensure desirability.

Negotiations are scheduled in two basic ways: in the time alloted for negotiations and in the time the parties are expected to adhere to the resolution of terms before negotiations will begin again. The alloted time may be scheduled either by a sequential process or by a temporal span; or a combination of both. The allotments of *temporal span* are easily applied to negotiations where both the terms and the sequential process of arriving at them are simple and fairly clear. In being hired for most kinds of employment where salary scales, levels of competence, and work conditions are standardized, only short scheduled periods — perhaps only a few moments — are alloted to negotiations. For example, only fifteen minutes may be given for the initial interview, then the candidate returns for a short discussion about the jobs available, and then his decision is expected in a prescribed amount of time. The decision to hold a mentally disturbed person on a 72-hour observation may have been determined in only five minutes of court time.

Sometimes the negotiations start out on a *strictly sequential basis* with the expectation that as much time as needed will be taken to get through an initial prescribed sequence. That completed, the remainder of the sequence is highly scheduled. This phenomenon occurs in purchasing homes and automobiles, in taking a subcontractors job, in signing up for a course. The buyer is allowed by his salesman to take all the time he wishes as the client is guided through phone calls, site visits, and tests. Once the client is determined to go on with his purchase, job, or commitment, the negotiation is focused on working out schedules, which will terminate the passage where compromise is adhered to within the span of time. The escrow is closed, the car delivered, the job proceeds on schedule, the course commences. Of course, if the sequential phase lasts too long there may be no time left for scheduling the finish of a passage, and the passagee may miss the passage altogether or have to wait until it comes around again.

In short, the efforts of the passagee and, particularly, of the agent are to change a negotiation, begun on sequential process which has unlimited time, to an alloted temporal span. They do this to bring about closure and commitment on a mutually desirable schedule. Sometimes this never occurs, as in strike negotiations or in the perennial search for a house that the purchaser never really intends to buy. Otherwise, a temporal span prescribing closure in any event may be built into the passage, as a limit against undue negotiations or to force emergence of a resolution in less than fruitful negotiations. In either case, the scheduled temporal span to force closure on negotiations occurs when people are resigned to compromise and to settling for less, because the loss through undue sequential processing becomes more than they can bear when they do not wish to lose a desirable passage.

The question then becomes: when should the participants in a passage begin to review and revamp compromises to insure its continued mutual desirability? Part of making an end to negotiations is to establish an answer to this question. One resolution is a contract for a stated period of time, after which new negotiations start automatically. Another resolution is a *scheduled periodic review* of the passage to see if new negotiations are warranted for bringing inequities for either agent or passagee back into balance. These reviews are typical in organizational careers. There is periodic review of perform-

ance to see if salaries or ranks should be raised or lowered commensu-
rate with changes in performance, age, or seniority; exceptional people should not be lost because the normal career does not reward them
enough, nor should incompetence be rewarded by normal career
progressions.

Until the periodic review or abstract termination is actually due,
both passagee and agents are assumed to consider the passage desirable enough to stick it out until negotiations are opened again. Consequently, needed but temporally early negotiations over new terms
may have to be forced by strikes, walkouts, or threats to quit the
passage. Otherwise, the party with more favorable terms may wish to
wait for the periodic review of the termination of a contract before
allowing new negotiations, because these in all likelihood will lower
the degree of desirability of the passage for a favored party.

In short, *the schedule of the passage regarding frequency of legitimate negotiations may constitute a favor for one and a delay for
another, when inequities in desirability develop in the course of shaping
the passage.* For example, as profits rise, Labor is always feeling that
Industry is getting the better of them out of the last wage and benefit
contract, but Labor does wait for the next period of negotiation.
Subcontractors who find their costs running somewhat higher than
expected will wait until the billing period after the job is over to
negotiate "extras." (If the costs run too high, however, they may stop
the job.) Banks with loans out that are unfavorable to them will wait
until the loan is due before increasing interest rates or instituting a
payoff schedule. During the periods of change in business cycles,
banks make the duration of loans as short as possible (three months
compared to six or twelve in stable times) to raise the frequency with
which lending passages can be negotiaged.

RECAPITULATIONS

Desirable status passages are subject to recapitulations by passagee and agents for several reasons — which in turn are based on two
general purposes: a combination of a sentimental journey back to
reenjoy aspects of the passage and to control either the forward shape
of the same or a new passage. Because both the purposes and the
reasons behind them are so intertwined we shall discuss the sentimen-

tal recapitulation first, and build up to the complexity of the interconnected expressive and instrumental factors involved.

Pure sentimental recapitulations of a passage occur under several social conditions. One condition that is brought about purposively is the reunion of a group or "class." People get together with their old cronies to relive, through talk and sociability, a passage that all found highly rewarding. They trade stories of fond memories. They recreate momentarily the pleasurable aspects of the passage, so that it will live on in the hearts of all who are attending the reunion. Thus, the former passage is resurrected and recapitulated on an annual basis that lasts but a single evening or weekend. This annual ceremony indicates how the passage left such deep pleasurable impressions that these necessitate an enjoyable revival — a connection between now and then.

Recapitulations during the reunion carefully avoid, ignore, or gloss over undesirable aspects of the passage, making it even more desirable in retrospect than perhaps it was. Classically, this is so in reunions of participants who in former adventures endured hardships and uncertainties. In reliving a sailing cruise, for instance, former crew companions take great pleasure in dwelling on completion of the passage (survival) and turn undesirable aspects of the passage such as storms and deprivations into hair-raising fun — enjoyable near misses of appalling catastrophy. Listening to such recapitulations with an unbiased ear, one can truly wonder if there were any desirable moments at all, save completing the passage itself. Thus, to some degree the desirability of the passage is a product of collective reviewal.[6]

Two other social conditions occasioning pure recapitulation are funerals and retirement ceremonies. During these, the relevant past passage may easily be eulogized by former co-passagees and agents. The eulogy need not be correct; its function is to exaggerate desirable aspects of the passage while avoiding both its undesirable aspects and its completion. Completion can only be mentioned as desirable if the next passage is desirable — as for the exhausted retiring person who needs a change. The funeral eulogy, of course, refers to the man's desirable life, not to a fatal illness. For both death and retirement, the eulogy settles accounts for the passagee on a happy note — with benign falsifications. His job may have been a bore, but the ceremony

6. M. Halbwachs, *Les Cadres Socialix de la Memoire* (Paris: Alcan, 1925).

brings out his long faithful service and a career marked by achievements and success. Mistakes and failures are omitted. Agents honor retiring men with medals, watches, or other symbols that underscore appreciation of the desirability of the passages both to passagees and agents. The retiring person is further supported by fellow colleagues who derive support for the desirability of their own passages — which will proceed toward similar honored completions.

Other occasions on which sentimental returns abound are the ordinary breaks that occur in daily interactions and activities. To pass the time, participants trade reminiscences of past enjoyable passages. Indeed, there easily occurs a competition to "one up" each other with a good story about a passage — say, at school or at play. The desire to compete well tends to distort favorably the desirability of a passage. Routine breaks at work occur, of course, during trips to the water fountain, at coffee time and lunches, and at brief encounters during all kinds of social occasions. People pass time enjoyably by telling and sharing what they have enjoyed. The recapitulations bring catharsis for oneself and contact with others. Much sociability is based on tiny recapitulations of desirable passages (and some not so desirable). But, unlike occasions for reunions, retirements and funerals, there is no formal or honoring ceremony. The similarity between formal and informal occasions consists of making an abstraction and an aggrandizement of desirability from the many details of the passage.

The less than pure sentimental journey back over a passage involves also an instrumental purpose, usually to derive from the review some means for controlling a current or newly generated passage. The most general aim is simply an effort to legitimate existing controls used in the present with which a passagee is unhappy, by giving or reminding the passagee of its positive, pleasurable tradition. It was beneficient then, and will be now: the past's claim on the present shape is worthy — so the rhetoric goes.

Controls may, however, be needed for application to several specific aspects of the passage to maintain its desirability. The reviewers may seek guides for managing *critical junctures* that either may occur again or will occur in a new passage. Desirable aspects of control will be used again or new controls figured out and, if possible, undesirable controls avoided. For example, how two parents handle the wedding of their daughter to ensure mutual desirability may partly be affected by how their own wedding was handled, and how their siblings' weddings were handled (when they themselves participated as agents).

Another aspect of the review is *discovering the nature of the desirable passage's antecedents which formerly required no control but do now — and vice versa.* Timing and strategies of controls now can be figured out to preserve under new circumstances the former desirability of the passage. Today, parents are trying to find controls over dating among teenagers that will reduce temptations leading to pregnancy or to the use of marijuana. Useful past controls may be abandoned when they are seen as no longer preserving desirability of the passage because of its changed direction and conditions. School children may be encouraged to work at their own levels rather than constrained to work at the class level, a decision in line with new directions in education. Or, in instituting a new university department, an effort is made to maximize the desirability of student passages by abandoning wherever possible those traditional controls that would dampen the passages — and perhaps always did.

One sentimental return that yields clear instrumental benefit is to *consult a former control agent* for aid in controlling the present. The agent may be interviewed about desirable aspects of the passage when he was involved, and so helps with ideas about current control. He may even be rehired — providing he will return and is likely to be a positive influence — to help insure the continued desirability of the present passage. By recapitulating, he may provide a model for recruiting a new control agent. Even after his retirement he may also provide a model to transcend or a negative model for recruiting new agents to keep the passage desirable and under control. By *negative* is meant that his once desirable style of control now is potentially undesirable, as both the passage and the conditions under which it occurs are changing. The classic example for all these possibilities is the regular consultation of former heads of organizations, whether industrial or governmental, partly for honorary and partly for advisory reasons (the latter is easily discounted).

Similarly, there can be *sentimental journeys with instrumental intent back to former contexts and arenas of a passage:* scrutinizing them for former norms, props, and attendant people to add to the current context for controlling the passage.

Maintaining continuity during change of the present passage is a primary reason for instituting sentimental-instrumental recapitulations about the desirable features of the past passages. This compara-tive perspective between past and present gives agents and passagees a greater insight into the desirability of specific current changes and continuities — as they guide the present and project or plan the future of the present passage. Its continued forward thrust may require such continual reviews into at least the short-term past, for supporting the present and giving direction at least to the. short-term future.

Passages that move slowly require fewer reviews, or at least at shorter intervals. Thus, doctors involved in quickly moving illness trajectories (heart attacks) may have daily conferences, while those involved in long-range trajectories have quarterly conferences Corporations that do simple jobs requiring only set policies may be content with annual conferences of stockholders and directors, to describe the past year and explain how fruitful the next will be, in continuity with slight changes which will be maintained.

Whatever the rate of the passage, whether quick or slow, such reviews for continuity with change not only provide control directly but provide it indirectly through the sentimental journey. Desirable sentiments thus revealed will support the current sentimental order and provide support for the continued movement (and shape) forward. This support is necessary for underwriting viable continued controls over the passage. Without the support, controls do not work well with agents or passagees, who may avoid, ignore, or rebel against them.

In sum, these regularized reviews — for control of continuity and change — involve an important, temporal dancing back and forth over the passage. The claims of the past on the present and future shape of the passage are scrutinized in an effort to make explicit the otherwise implicit claims to desirable aspects of the passage. Various aspects of passage then can be guided and continued or be terminated according to these claims.

Some recapitulations of a desirable passage are strictly instrumental — no sentimental purpose is involved. The purpose of these recapitulations is to discover where the desirable passage went wrong or broke down. *Critical review* is made of a once desirable passage to fix fault, negligence, or blame, or to find a way to patch up the passage so that it becomes desirable again for the passagee, agent, and others. This reviewal may become part of a lawsuit, as when business or marital partners wish to separate and then to gain something from the other who is accused of having been harmful to the once desirable passage. A critical review may occur when scrutinizing a dropout from school; the effort is made to patch up the passage if possible or prevent such an undesirable end from happening to others in like passage. A critical reviewal occurs just before an undesirable demotion (after its announcement) in a career, and whenever children rebel and leave parents. Both examples suggest that other agents (colleagues, wives, social workers, and judges) may also enter into the critical review.

While it is begun with no sentiment, this critical review can arouse enough sentiment to turn it into a partial sentimental journey. Especially is this true when the review is over a marital, familial, or work passage, because these central passages usually have a deep effect on the passagee or agents. Unless the review becomes an effort to reconstitute the passage to its previous desirable state, the sentiments become at least partly discounted in favor of realistic assessment of its current undesirable features and also, if pertinent, discounted by the desire to blame and receive compensation at the expense of the other. Thus, the critical review of a once desirable passage may produce a highly critical juncture, when it is ascertained once and for all that passage is now undesirable both to passagees and agents. Such a critical review delineates how and why the mutually desirable passages break down.

Undesirable For Passagee

When the status passage is desirable only for the agent, then recalcitrance and conflict are likely to dominate it. Whether the agent tries to *persuade* the passagee to cooperate or *forces* him to go along with the passage depends upon the kind of power he has at hand and whether the situation is appropriate for its use. Usually, the agent possesses a combination of powers for gaining some measure of compliance and cooperation. He has the ability to gain the passagee's attention at certain times, when he can communicate at will. He tries to persuade, convince, and convert. In his temporal ordering of these efforts at conversion he will try to include the right atmosphere or situation conducive to conversion. Agents of an institution, such as guards in prisons and attendants in mental institutions, may hold group conferences or thereapy sessions with prisoners, patients, or inmates respectively to gain their cooperation. They, also, may have private consultations. They encourage cooperation as a way of making the passage less undesirable for the passagee.

When efforts at conversion or persuasion fail, usually some agents, particularly institutional ones, are able to use powers of enforcement based on physical or normative forces. A prisoner can be put into solitary confinement. (A political or war prisoner, in some countries, may even be killed.) Host agents can revoke privileges or induce hardships of various sorts and degrees to gain cooperation. Children can be spanked, students suspended or expelled, "noncooperative" patients in the hospital reprimanded or their complaints and requests ignored. Thus, when agents control the reward system that controls desirability of a passage, they can discourage or encourage behaviors through this reward system so that the passagee will cooperate more during an undesirable passage. The passagee's only resort may be to halt his passage through such tactics as striking or dropping out. For the inmates of many institutions such tactics may be difficult; these persons are captive passagees of inevitable passages no matter how undesirable. (They can only mitigate undesirability through such tactics as described in the chapter on Shape.)

While ordinarily *the recovery passage* (from illness) is desirable for both the patient and the doctor, under certain conditions this passage is desirable only for the agent — neither the process nor goal of the passage seems desirable to the passagee. The basic condition for this situation is that the patient does not realize he is sick or can deny it, because he has no particular pain or other recognizable symptoms (as in many heart, psychiatric, or tuberculosis cases). Thus, he believes it undesirable to submit to the regimen, often rigorous and costly, of a recovery passage that seems meaningless or of low priority. Because the agent believes, however, that the passage is desirable, he tries to convince the passagee of this while simultaneously using what means he has to enforce the requisite cooperation for treatment. The means of enforcement vary from simple, authoritarian efforts by the doctor, to family pressures and legal controls as in tuberculosis or mental disease. The result is further strain, and resentment or even a sense of betrayal on the part of the passagee.[7]

Another less prevalent condition making the recovery passage undesirable for a patient is the *source of his illness* — this may cause trouble with family and friends, stigmatize or de-value him. If cooperation during the recovery passage results in the illness being made public, then the passage becomes undesirable and the patient will be recalcitrant about engaging in it. If an executive or a doctor has a bad heart, and if this is known, it can devalue him for his work. Publicizing his condition by making him adhere to a strict regimen might penalize him occupationally or financially. Similarly, a person with a legal problem may see passage through the courts as stigmatizing; therefore, lawyers dislike instituting a suit for a client who can be harmed, because the suit is bad for both the client and for the lawyer's future business.

When concealment is sufficiently possible in such situations, a passagee will be more cooperative with agents, for he can make the passage without too much social risk. Thus, in a closed awareness context, recovery passages may become desirable for both passagee and agent, and the agent also will try his best to maintain concealment to retain the passagee's cooperation (as in the public health enforcement of treatment for venereal disease). Should concealment fail, the passagee might break out, drop out, or disappear — even commit suicide — or become a recalcitrant passagee to publicize his denial of what others are forcing him through.

The *degree or inevitability of choice* the passagee has while going through the recovery passage will also affect how desirable he sees it, and therefore how he must be managed. If a TB patient must go to the hospital for a cure, the legal compulsion itself probably will make the passage undesirable. Compounding this is his being plucked from normal life and perhaps by his not feeling ill. Recovering from some illness that does allow some degree of progressive freedom to the passagee may reduce the undesirability of the passage. As it progresses, undesirability may decrease still further if its stigmatizing aspects can be concealed — however slightly if affects reputation,

7. Erving Goffman, "The Moral Career of the Mental Patient," in *Asylums* (Chicago: Aldine Publishing Co., 1961), pp. 125-171. Anselm L. Strauss *et al., Psychiatric Institutions and Ideologies* (New York: The Free Press, 1964).

physical stamina, or financial liquidity — providing that a favorable recovery is sure to be complete and on schedule (that is, the shape is certain). The same propositions apply to lawsuits. People who are forced into lawsuits find them highly undesirable: people choosing them, presumably have a high probability of winning, and find the undesirability less burdensome.

When the degree of choice does not remain constant throughout the passage, this affects the perceived undesirability. It is true that if a passagee is being forced but does begin to recover, then if the force keeping him in passage is reduced he is likely to stay with the passage — however if recovery is not occurring, or seems not worthwhile, then the passagee's tendency is to break out of passage. Agents who force an undesirable passage take into account this potential loss of a passagee when adjusting his degree of freedom to stay with the passage. This problem is, of course, perennial for doctors.

Even when not allowing complete choice, agents adjust the degree of choice that pertains to voluntariness or inevitability of the passage on its various dimensions. Depending on the particular passage, the passagee is given freedom regarding matters such as work schedules, living space, leisure activities, and diet. The prison inmate is allowed to type until 10:00 p.m. or take work furloughs. An inmate of a mental hospital may roam the grounds and even be permitted "home visits" occasionally. Hospital patients choose their own diets. Soldiers are given weekend passes. Defendants are permitted to plead guilty to lesser charges.[8] Students can waive required courses if they achieve well enough elsewhere.

It is apparent that the fate of a passagee — in a passage he believes undesirable but his agents find desirable — will depend considerably both on the kind of inevitability of the passage and whether the agents are the source of inevitability. In both instances an agent can attempt to decrease the undesirability; but only if he can control its inevitability can he give the passagee enough freedom to break out of the passage or make parts of it desirable. Otherwise, the agent can only ameliorate what a law court, a higher authority, a life cycle, or an illness will inevitably do to the passagee — the passage continues as undesirable.

8. David Sudnow, "Normal Crimes," *Social Problems* (Winter 1965) Vol. 12, No. 3, pp. 255-276.

Sometimes a passagee enters a passage believing it desirable but discovers that neither passage nor its goal is desirable. One source of this mistaken entry is lack of knowledge about, or criteria by which to evaluate the passage beforehand; meanwhile, a push into passage is provided by general values that indicate the desirability of such types of passage. In view of such possible undesirabilities as a job or career that does not work out or a marriage that collapses, some people may make test runs or spend time trying to foresee the future. These pre-passage tactics become more important and intensified when a person knows that, once it has begun, to break out of an actual passage will be difficult. If breaking out will not be difficult (say, a weekend dalliance at an out-of-town convention), people take chances on the unknown more easily.

Often the potential passage cannot really be known accurately. Because this is so, one might try to improve on his prediction by looking at models, although, in fact, the models also may be questionable. Sometimes the potential passage conceivably can be sufficiently known — many professional and organizational careers — but the passagee beforehand remains unaware of it because he lacks resources for knowing, or he is unaware of where to get the requisite information.

Another source of entry into the unknown (where desirability is the anticipation and undesirability is the eventuality) is being persuaded, sold, conned, or convinced by another passagee or by an agent. Passagees continually do this to the unsuspecting (misery loves company). To offset his own undesirable passage, the passagee proselytizes it as desirable, gaining feedback thereby about its desirability by obtaining fellow passagees.[9] In the world of investment, investors who are experiencing losses frequently need others to share the ride down. As for agents, of course we are all aware of sales pitches, which get people into passages that later prove undesirable for them but quite desirable for the agents. The con game is only an extreme example; the sales of deficient products is a more ordinary example.

Agents in such voluntary — yet to become undesirable — passages engage in hooking processes. Two basic hooking tactics are to misrepresent the passage's undesirable factors and to bait the prospec-

9. Leon Festinger *et al., When Prophecy Fails* (Minneapolis: University of Minnesota, 1956), pp. 58-87.

tive passagee with promises of monetary, financial, psychological, physical, or temporal gain. The con man promises money, the salesman promises satisfactions, and the subcontractor promises quick action. Once the passage has begun, the agent juggles circumstances as best he can to keep prominent the passage's desirable features. Also, he monopolizes as much as possible all information on current happenings, while covering by assuring the passagee he is serving him by keeping control and watching over "things." He continually baits, saying favorable prospects are coming soon. When the passagee is firmly hooked, with limited or no capability to break out of the passage, then the agent can relax his tactics and pretenses.

After achieving their goals from the passagee, some agents may walk out on the passagee, leaving him to extricate himself as best he can. For example, after obtaining a client's signature on a sales contract, a salesman may disappear with his commission leaving the client to deal with the problems of securing the promised product or service. (At this point, the voluntary passage changes in some degree to an involuntary one.) The breaking out of a passagee may vary considerably: say, from simply leaving but with some penalty, accepting the discomforts and inevitability of a bad deal but engaging in "internal exile," to hiring a lawyer to extricate oneself, to going through a degradation ceremony in order to get out, to illegally breaking out (going AWOL), or finally to committing suicide. A crucial condition in all this is the stake that the passagee has in relation to stakes in his other passages and the degree of discomfort or pain of remaining in the undesirable passage when some "out" is really possible.

The progressive undesirability of a passage is one natural course of entry into an undesirable passage. In these cases, we need no longer refer to what the passagee could have known beforehand. After the passage turns bad, awareness of this follows not far behind — as in a desired pregnancy which turns progressively bad. Such undesirability varies by degree. The normal degree of undesirability in a pregnancy involves some increase of discomfort — nausea, heartburn, backache, clumsiness, diet deprivation, fewer positions of comfort — and a lowering of self-image as bodily disfigurement increases. Usually, the doctor and husband will still consider the outcome of the pregnancy desirable and support her through its strain. Sometimes severe problems develop that also make these agents consider the pregnancy undesirable; they might then support a quick end to this passage by abortion. Similarly, when stocks drop in market value, a broker might suggest to his investor selling out quickly to reduce "the damage."

Two other sources of entry into an undesirable passage are *force* and *threat.* For penalizing passages — a prison term — these sources of entry are obvious. It is assumed sometimes that the implicit threat of imprisonment is a deterrant to breaking the law. Other forms of threat are ostracization or physical and psychological abuse that can push a person into undesirable passages. Thus, through normal "group-process," a student may be inducted into drug use or induced to drop out of high school before graduating to get a job for quick cash needed to keep up with the style of his peers.

As a passagee becomes hooked into a progressively undesirable passage, his tendency is to fix responsibility, perhaps to seek retribution for damages, and to find a way to break out of the passage. His passage may also become progressively undesirable for an agent, who then may wish to get rid of this particular passagee to avoid blame and damages to his own reputation. (Of course, if many of his passagees become dissatisfied then the agent may quit overseeing such passages altogether.) Thus, we have variations of degree whereby a passage which becomes undesirable for the passagee can thereby become undesirable for the agent.

Let us take a frequently found example of this process in the client-expert relationship. As time passes and results are lacking, costs mounting, and perhaps even some damage done to person or property, a client may become dissatisfied with his expert. A desirable passage clearly has become undesirable, but simultaneously the client is becoming progressively hooked into it. Hooking occurs through the normal development of a joint history of experience, and a file to document it. The file has value in and of itself to the client: this value lies in the cost — in time, money, understanding, and effort — necessary for developing another joint history with a new expert. The passagee may have become quite dissatisfied long before giving up this joint history with his expert. His dissatisfaction may take a long time to evolve if the expert-client relationship follows the typical pattern of periods of long time occurring between meetings necessary to obtain and give service.

Once the passagee has decided perhaps to terminate the passage, he starts by holding the expert responsible for the undesirability of what has and is happening. He may complain, or accuse the expert verbally, or in written form, threatening termination unless matters are put to rights. This is the beginning of an *announcement of departure* and often the beginning of the agent's belief that for him, also, the passage is now undesirable. The passagee can skip the pre-announcement and simply announce departure, if he thinks beneficial changes will not occur by remaining longer. Perhaps usually a client makes a degree of announcement, because he would like to give his expert some chance to redress grievances. Alternatively, the client may merely *drift away* as his dissatisfaction leads him (or his friends or kinsmen persuade him) to seek another expert or to give up altogether this type of passage. The agent may never even know of the passage's termination. In announced instances — let alone unannounced — the client may be unable (especially with doctors, lawyers, and accountants) to take his file with him. Even if he can, his new expert is likely to discount it in favor of starting his own from scratch. Although they have legitimate reasons for doing that, the client, of course, pays the price of acquiring that new file. Even when leaving the tutelage of a piano teacher, the student may suffer some monetary loss because his new teacher assigns different musical compositions or books of exercises.

Upon receipt of an announcement of dissatisfaction, and accusations that he is less than responsible having made errors of omission or commission, the expert will decide whether to let the client go or try to hold him. If the situation has become too undesirable, or is of negligible moment to the agent, his tendency is to allow severance — and, if the passagee will not leave, then to get rid of him by increasing his dissatisfaction or discomfort through inattention, confession of inability to do anything, or accusing the client also of irresponsibility.

But, if the expert finds a degree of undesirability occurring that puts his competence in doubt, and especially if it threatens his public reputation or esteem, he will attempt to forestall the client's departure. He does so especially when afraid of a lawsuit, or of "blackball" referrals or subtle informal attacks occurring among his colleagues on his expertise. Lawyers and doctors continually face this problem. An expert may engage in many tactics singly or in combination. He points to his and the client's initial history, and to his original sincere offer to see the case or job through to a positive conclusion. He then asks for a chance to redress the difficulties that plague the client's case. In effect, he gives a promissory note, whose terms are that if things get no better within the alloted time each will consent to breaking their relationship. Also, he probably will promise immediate personal adjustments (as in attention) and situational adjustments (as in office procedures or teaching methods) or whatever he believes will partly satisfy the client's complaints. He may, however, choose to "go on the aggressive" and claim superior insight into what is really happening, as when a gynecologist told a long-suffering and obviously not improving lady of our acquaintance that she had not enough patience — and besides she ought to see a psychiatrist because some of her obstetrical problem must be mental.

The expert will also, if feasible in his particular case, warn about the potential harm in leaving at midstream. When he gives such a warning, the expert thereby tampers with the trust involved in their relationship, for in telling about the dangers of switching experts or leaving the passage together, if it appears that the dangers are unreal, the client is likely to distrust the expert further. If the dangers seem real, however, the client will feel locked into a passage he cannot advisedly leave — which again increases its undesirability. Yet, under this condition he may temporarily renew his trust in the expert and cease accusations or recriminations in the interest of trying again.

Also, in pointing to their mutual history the expert may suggest a consultation with an outside expert that is tantamount to evaluating his own expertise and the "true" undesirability of his client's passage. The expert may also draw upon friendship with his client to smooth over or obfuscate difficulties. Many a client will be too guilty to walk out on a friend even if the friend acting as expert seems to be giving unsatisfactory service.

If the expert wishes to maintain his reputation with the client by redressing undesirable features of the case, yet wishes to be rid of the client, he can suggest a lack of fit in their relationship and recommend that a colleague take over. The expert also may suggest the client go elsewhere for service, while assuring him that he can always return for consultation or continued service again.

In such an undesirable passage the client is vulnerable to solicita-

tion by other experts, unless professional agreements against solicitation exist. As the new expert "sniffs" problems while talking to a potential client, he can easily remark how in his office or practice these problems are handled with the client's comfort and fate in mind. In short, this expert invites him to abandon his old agent; then he and the client together will make the new passage "as it should be." Insofar as such raiders often are around, some clients develop the pattern of making the rounds seeking a more knowledgeable expert than their current ones. Raiding and openness to raiding are characteristic features of all service trades.

At other times, a *client may be altogether talked out of a type of passage* by friends and family, or by other types of experts. He is told he does not really need an architect, an accountant, a psychiatrist, a specialist for his problem — so why put up with such an unhappy present situation. He may also decide to give up the activity altogether, or attempt to be his own expert. The do-it-yourself boom (in medicine, hardware stores, and tool rentals) is designed to make passagees act as their own agents, bringing them satisfactions in doing their own job and avoiding present or future costs and time wasted with experts.

Passage Undesirable For Agent

When the status passage is desirable only for the passagee, negotiating with and convincing the agent to take on control and to stay with the passage will characterize their relationship. Temporal and directional aspects of a passage can dissuade potential agents from taking on types of passage. For example, the night-time and lengthy hours involved in obstetrics dissuade many a physician from being an obstetrician. Men shy from work on the police force or fire department because of the danger and the hours involved. Also, the context of passage may dissuade an agent from taking on a passage. Thus teachers may not wish to teach in an all black school or in a lower quality institution or in a politically or religiously different institution. Getting the potential agent to take on the passage takes convincing and negotiating over conditions and over a career that will please him.

An agent may also not wish to take on particular passagees because aspects of them make the passages undesirable. Thus, schools screen students for desirable attributes, to prevent undesirable pass-agees from entering. Once a student has been accepted, he will find certain potential advisors either steering clear or willing to work with him for reasons (yet or forever unknown) to him. The reasons may vary from a lack of fit between the two persons, to so great a current work load for the advisor that he must avoid spreading himself too thin. Professionals thus will avoid clients with whom they feel a lack of fit or for whom they have no time, thereby avoiding an undesirable passage for themselves.

To get a potential agent to take on a passagee requires a process of convincing and negotiating that is different from taking on a pass-agee. The latter process requires provision of working conditions and a career that will satisfy the passagee. The former process requires convincing the potential agent that the passagee has what it takes to go through a passage in a desirable manner. The process of convincing and its attendant negotiating requires bringing prospects in a credible way to the reluctant, potential agent's attention. The passagee may have a means and access to do it himself or may have to depend on a sponsor. The agent must be convinced with some surety that the passagee can go somewhere (as in an organizational career), make the grade (as in learning a musical instrument), or be able to pay well (as in a referral to an extremely busy lawyer). As an alternative, he may be able to make the grade as a promising client just because certain of his attributes are appealing to the potential agent — an "interesting medical case" for the physician or a precedent-setting legal case for the lawyer.

Once taken on, the passagee is *on trial* with his agent, who can usually bring the passage to a truncated end by quitting if it proves undesirable. The agent's ability to escape after the trial period is usually formally obtained when he takes on a passagee by contract. After this trial period, the responsibility of guiding the shape of the passage makes it harder for the agent to break out of the passage if it subsequently turns bad. He will be expected by others, and usually by himself, to see the job through to some finish before actually leaving the passage. Thus, teachers leave a school at the end of the school year, not during it. Piano teachers give the poor student a reasonable time before washing their hands of him. However, seeing the passage partly through does not usually preclude planning a departure beforehand. The agent tells others his schedule for leaving so he can be replaced — with no loss of an institution's control over a passage or with little loss of time or money to the passagee — and so he himself will not be harmed thereafter.

The Undesirable Passage

A major source of an undesirable passage for both agent and passagee is that which *turns undesirable because of a reversal or a critical* incident that changes its direction. We have had examples such as the natural reversal in a marriage, or the critical incident of further illness despite the physician's best efforts, or contextual change, such as reverses in the economy or a market which make an investment go sour for both broker and investor. For both agent and passagee the question then arises of how soon and in what manner one can break out or end or redirect the passage, and whether the passage is inevitable.

In some cases — particularly in illness passages — the people involved feel that the less said about the passage to all concerned the better, until it is over. These passages are kept secrets as much as possible. At the other extreme is the degradation ceremony, which emphasizes the end to a very undesirable passage for all concerned.[10] The awareness context is fully opened, the undesirable details announced for all to hear. This kind of event occurs in courtrooms and with some frequency in the military service. The anticipated consequences of such disclosures are a reaffirming of the moral order and, hopefully, a deterrent of other passagees and agents from allowing such undesirable circumstances to reoccur.

Such deterrence is doubtful, however, because the conditions that lead into an undesirable passage are not so amenable to control of direction and time by either passagee or agent — or they would have prevented the problem. Examples of such conditions are illness, neuroticism, impulsive behavior, or marital problems — any or all of which may have turned a student's career sour for both him and his sponsors. Although both may try to exert control over these circumstances, they can fail and fail badly.

10. Harold Garfinkel, "Conditions of Successful Degradation Ceremonies," *American Journal of Sociology* (1956), 61: pp. 420-24.

Recapitulations of undesirable passages are held to a minimum, because dwelling on them is also experienced as undesirable. The details are best forgotten and not remembered. Recapitulations do occur when an effort is made to fix blame, as in a lawsuit or a governmental inquiry, or to find a chain of events that can lead either to a rereversal or to preventing another such passage from being so undesirable. Such recapitulations are *purely instrumental.* Recapitulations with a sentimental purpose of a reversal in a once desirable passage can have turned sour. Then the participants might have the strength to review how good it once was, particularly if the good old days, or at least earlier days, help to handle current misery. This condition, for example, occurs during dying passages and in the downward mobility of once thriving prostitutes,[11] and even after divorces.

People who participate as agents and passagees in devalued (*i.e.* socially undesirable) passages will generally hesitate to look back if they believe them devalued. This is the case with lowly occupations or jobs such as those of tenant farmers, janitors, kitchen workers, maids, where reviewals of one's situation probably are rare and expectations of leaving are slight because of lack of actual or perceived alternative or social leverage or because of personal inertia.

As we remarked earlier, the *probability of a rereversal is ascertained often by an instrumental recapitulation,* which sets forth how the undesirable reversal occurred (and perhaps even a previous rereversal). This occurs in alcoholism. The recapitulation sets forth how the person became an alcoholic so that the conditions producing this direction in his passage can be altered and the passage reversed. If the alcoholic had already been cured, but a critical incident or agent in his life had started him on drink again, the rereversal (recidivism) is reviewed to ascertain how to reinstitute a desirable recovery — such as getting him reinvolved with AA and with specific members of it.

It should be obvious from our discussion that an undesirable passage for both agent and passagee is likely to have adverse effects on their other passages. Troublesome undesirable passages tend to take time as the participants attempt to correct them. These passages

11. See James H. Bryan, "Apprenticeships in Prostitution," *Social Problems* (Winter, 1965) Vol. 12, No. 3, pp. 287-297 and "Occupational Ideologies of Call Girls," *Social Problems* (Spring, 1966) Vol. 13, No. 4, pp. 441-50.

demoralize, and this may slow activity elsewhere. Also they may stigmatize the person, hence affect his other passages.[12] In contrast, desirable passages do not carry these burdens, and so, while they may adversely affect other passages, they do not affect them in the same manner.

12. Erving Goffman, *Stigma* (Englewood Cliffs, N. J.: Prentice Hall, Inc., 1963).

6. PASSAGES: COLLECTIVE, AGGREGATE, AND SOLO

AMONG THE structural conditions that profoundly affect the nature and consequences of status passages are those pertaining to the numbers of agents and passagees, in combination with the respective relationships of all concerned. The simplest visualization of how important those conditions can be is to imagine the differences (both to passagees and agents) of whether someone goes through passage in concert with others rather than as a solo passagee.

The following variable structural conditions can usefully be conceived as a grid of possibilities. Persons can go through a passage (1) *alone,* (2) as a member of a *cohort* that develops a collective or group character, or (3) as a member of an *aggregate* that has minimal collective features. Looking now at status passages from the perspective of the agent, agents can operate *alone,* as members of *collectivities,* or less usually in *aggregate* fashion. Because both agents and passagees can operate in multiple contexts, analytically the possible combinations are nine in number. Each combination of structural conditions has its own set of major contingent issues.

116

In this chapter, we shall be concerned especially with collective —collective relationships, solo-solo relationships, solo-collective relationships, and to a lesser extent with variations in the aggregate relationships. A moment's thought about the preceding chapters reminds us both that contents of this present one have been foreshadowed and that the sets of conditions at its focus are greatly affected by variables discussed earlier.

Collective-Colle~tive

When collective-collective conditions obtain, both agents and passagees have their own sets of contingent problems. What we shall call the *agent group* (a faculty of a school is one example), has at least three major problems. First, they are concerned with working out and maintaining a proper shape for the collective passage of the current passagee group. Second, they are concerned with the management of those individual passagees whose performances depart disturbingly from the normal ones dictated by the expected usual shape. Third, the agent group is concerned with articulating the passages of multiple cohorts of passagees who, at any moment, are at different steps in passage.

The passagees, in their turn, face two typical problems. First, they are concerned with achieving some measure of control over the shape of their collective passage. Second, they are concerned with gaining some control over their individual passages. Group interest and personal interests may support or run counter, depending on variable but determinable conditions, but the potential discrepancy between the two types of interest is inherent in group membership.

Status passages of this type typically occur on institutional or organizational terrains — medical schools, army camps, and monasteries. To put a cohort through its collective passage, there must be at least minimal organizational machinery, places to assemble as one group or as sections, agents to teach and control and, in common parlance, often requisite "materials" such as textbooks or prescribed readings or lectures or "work," which embody standardized tasks for the passagee to learn and from which he is taught.

Because there are multiple agents, there is always the possibility of divergent views about the most desirable shape of collective passage.

Internal dissention is minimized when the backgrounds (*i.e.,* recruitment) of agents are similar and when there is minimal differentiation
in their division of labor within the organization. Homogeneity of
perspectives with its consequent differential experience and characteristic generation of differential perspectives means maximum agreement about the desired shape of cohort passage. It also means that the
agents cannot easily be played off, one against another, by the passagees. Also, there is less likelihood that individual agents will covertly
maneuver against the intentions of the agent group. Another condition that tends toward maximizing homogeneity of views is the situation where the control of shape is largely in the hands of officers,
leaders, or "top management." Then, however, they must take steps
to guard against discrepant action by agents who do not agree with
their own ideas about the shape of either the collective passage or the
passages of particular individuals. Standard strategies for achieving
that internal control include elaborate or *ad hoc* spy systems and the
balancing of rewards and punishments. The ultimate punishments
may be dismissal or death.

When organizations are rent with dissention, marked by factions
competing for control of the organization and hence for control of
status passages, *then* passagees face *great opportunities* and *great
dangers.* A cohesive cohort of passagees may play off one group of
agents against another, to what they believe is their own collective
advantage. Even if the cohort does not act thus in concert, individuals
may manage to gain advantage from the dissention among agents. The
ultimate tragedy is when the ranks of both agents and passagees are
so splintered that the institution is brought not merely to a halt but
ends by going out of business. (The example that springs to mind
during 1969 when this chapter is being written, is that student demonstrations, a strike involving only part of the faculty, administrative
splits, all combined with public dissention, may destroy San Francisco
State College.) Another possibility, frequently seen in the history of
religious and political organizations, is sectarian splintering from the
main organization, with each faction then pursuing its own goals —
including the management of the status passages of its internal cohorts.

*Some of the strain of discrepant views about shape within organiza-
tions can be minimized when the pacing and steps of passages are less*

than rigorously prescribed and scheduled, allowing tolerance for divergence. A good example is that massive collective passage that occurred just after the Communist Revolution in China, when the government decreed everyone who was literate should join in a crash program to insure the quick attainment of literacy by the entire population. Although general guidelines were laid down, great latitude was permitted or developed in means, pacing, and so on because this was, after all, a great and ecstatic experiment. When an organization is new or becoming "revitalized" and can afford or even idealize its internal discrepancies of view, emergent or discoverable passages also are accompanied by fair latitude in the management of collective shape by individual agents or groups of agents.

There is also the possibility of trade-offs through segmentalization or specialization within the division of labor, as when some portion of a faculty is permitted virtual management of the undergraduates, while another set of faculty members works out the fate of the graduate students. When, however, undergraduates feed into the ranks of the graduates — that is, when these two passages are continuous rather than discontinuous — discrepancies in their shape will generally be reviewed, if not fought over. In such instances time enters in as a variable; because neither group may be aware of the consequences of their different managements of cohort shape until later, they are confronted with the consequential evidence.

It is worth adding that even rather scheduled or prescribed passages can permit some degree of latitude, either for less rigorously defined portions of the cohort passage or for aspects viewed as being least fateful by those agents in greatest control of the cohort passage. As the consequences of that latitude become better known, it is possible that tightened control may ensue or that more loosely defined phases of passage may be redefined in the direction of "more important," therefore more prescribed.

Parallel to that institutional machinery is a greater or lesser degree of cohesiveness — and so a potential for action in its own perceived behalf — of the passagee group. A long history of association combined with traditional roots in kinship and community yield maximum conditions for cohesiveness that may operate against either totally undesirable passages (decreed, for instance, by governments) or, less drastically, against undesirable aspects of a generally desirable passage. Resistances toward collectivization by Chinese and Russian peasants are classic examples of the effectiveness of traditional bases of cohesiveness. Agents who attempt to handle such resistant cohesiveness may use various strategies, varying from force to gentle or gradual modes of persuasion. The consequences, as we all know, may vary from complete victory of the resistant group (virtual control of shape) or overthrow of the agent authority (completely victorious control).

Under certain institutional or organizational conditions, there may be less cohort cohesiveness, and indeed agents may utilize deliberate tactics to reduce or minimize *cohort contact* to minimize possibilities of such cohesiveness for purposes of maintaining, strengthening, or maximizing their own control over the collective passage. Conversely, if the agents are less fearful of opposition or the passage is proceeding smoothly, they may not think to utilize or devise such tactics, nor may they scrutinize spatial and temporal features of the organization that might further cohort cohesion. If they did, or when they do, they will find it expedient to change those features to minimize contact and communication among the passagees. Unless they take proper precautions, however, either to accomplish this with skill (including "reasonable" explanations to the passagees) or without the passagees really taking note of these important changes, resistance to the agent group's action is only likely to increase — with further escalation of determination by the cohort group, to gain greater control of its collective destiny.

The longer the cohort is in passage, the more likely it is to develop a consensus about what matters are of greatest moment for itself, unless of course countervailing conditions making for feuds or critical dissensus prevail. Even then, some measure of what in describing medical students Becker *et al.* termed *student culture* is likely to evolve.[1] Cohort culture arises, as studies such as Becker's or Olesen's and Whitaker's[2] make clear, primarily because the passagees face common contingencies. The more the passagees realize that those contingencies confront them all, the more they will share definitions

1. Howard S. Becker *et al, Boys in White* (Chicago: University of Chicago Press, 1961).

2. Virginia Olesen and Elvi Whittaker, *The Silent Dialogue* (San Francisco: Jossey-Bass, 1968).

about those contingencies as well as notions about how to cope with them. Also, the more contingencies, the more likely there is to arise a shared perspective compounded in some part, understandably, of a collective memory about past victories and defeats. Even when agents' control is very effective, lightly felt or judged genuinely benign, inevitably there will be small confrontations between the agent group and the cohort group. Tactics then are less radical or rash, negotiation more tactful and less strident. Yet all these contingencies help to form a measure of consensus — the groundwork for further cohesion if the confrontations become blunter.

The nature of these discrepancies of viewpoint between the sub-collectivities of agents and passagees rests not only on their different social position, but also on some of the variables discussed in earlier chapters. For instance, if the transitional statuses are perfectly clear and passage through them is well regulated and firmly scheduled, whatever disagreements (however minor) may evolve between agent and passagee groups are likely to evolve around the very clarity and regularity of the passage. The latter may wish to speed up or slow down a clearly defined transitional stage. Yet the more loosely regulated passages may result in negotiations and confrontations about making matters more precise, more regulated or scheduled or prescribed; or conversely, misunderstandings may grow up around just how loosely defined some steps in the passage really are, with confrontations ensuing over the agent group's sudden "tightening up" — and accusations about reneging or even double-crossing. Some agents may, on occasion, become scapegoats (reprimanded publicly or dismissed) in order that the agent group save face and not lose further control over the shape of the cohort passage.

In the above paragraphs, we have almost always assumed that passagees define their collective passage as *generally desirable.* What if they are deemed *undesirable?* Consider the plight of captured American soldiers interned in Korean (Chinese) prisoner-of-war camps. Authorities in these encampments bent their efforts toward "brainwashing" their prisoners. They used tactics such as attempting to deceive the Americans into believing their own officers and government had betrayed them, or spreading rumors that among the captured soldiers some had turned Communist and now were acting as spies for the prison authorities. The former tactic was countered by strong talking by the less vulnerable to more vulnerable prisoners. The rumors about spies were less easily manageable and eventuated in a considerable amount of what Biederman termed "mutual suspicion" among the interned men. In consequence, each tended to confide increasingly less in anyone else, and group solidarity was thereby lessened. Similarly, when prisoners plan to escape they do not tell all their other associates for fear that one among them may turn spy or actually be a "plant." Keeping the planned reversibility a secret enhances the probability of their escape but also enhances the probability that the remaining prisoners will fall under suspicion of abetting the escape, or will be punished anyhow, or made to submit now to more stringent rules to prevent their imitating the escapees.

Whether desirable or undesirable, the collective passage may not be entirely congruent in all its details with what individuals define as their personal interests. This is the second major contingency that arises when a cohort goes through a common passage. Inherent in group membership are actual or perceived discrepancies between personal and group versions of effective tactics and strategies, if not indeed between ideas about goals and basic values. In anthropological accounts of tribal rites that mark passage from adolescent to adult status, one gets the impression that discrepancies between individual and cohort are completely minimized[3] — although it needs to be recognized that logically, at least, potential discrepancy always exists. In effect, a collective passage always has solo passages embedded "within it."

It is safe to say that unless a collective passage is of very short duration and the passagees of very homogeneous background, there at least will be occasional strain among members of the cohort as they act on different ideas about how better to achieve personal ends while going through their collective passage. Discrepant views can, it is easy to understand, evolve over virtually all of the items of passage discussed in earlier chapters: shape, rate, scheduling, phasing, and so forth. Perhaps the more the differences in past experience and biography, the more likely are such discrepant views likely to arise and persist.

Whenever such discrepancies evolve and an individual acts in

3. Cf., W. L. Warner, *Black Civilization* (New York: Harper & Row, 1937).

accordance with his own viewpoint, he will have to face the consequences of his action, if visible, as seen by others in his cohort. His tactics may include, of course, keeping his action invisible to them or at least to all except others with very similar views. (Invisibility is furthered by structural features, such as the large size of the student body of a graduate department plus scattered classrooms and no central meeting place for students; or the division of labor in hospitals that keeps medical residents separated for many hours of the day.) At the other extreme, he may attempt to convert all others to his view of the aspect of passage under question, either because all will then benefit or more cynically because he at least will benefit.

That attempts to control aspects of one's personal passage lead to complex interactions among individuals in the cohort is another implication of solo "within" collective passage. Among the most consequential implications are *competition* among the passagees and *cooperation* among them. When cohesion of the group is great, virtually all members may cooperate in keeping competition minimal as well as insuring that laggards in pace are coached — or their true pace concealed from the agent group — so as neither to be reprimanded nor flunked out. Researchers (and brighter students) have noted that restricted competition combined with mutual aid penalizes the speedier — unless they conceal their pace and the work on which it may be based from colleagues.

The agent group also cannot avoid the reality that solo passages exist side-by-side with the collective passage, however much the agents wish to regard the cohort as a homogeneous unit. Only under exceptional circumstances, such as are involved in the ritual passages mentioned earlier, do moments inevitably arise during the collective passage when agents perceive actions by passagees that run counter to the desired shape of the passage. Both to control that shape and to prevent a deviant act from developing into a thoroughly deviant passagee, the agents will evolve appropriate tactics. They may exhort the individual, or warn and publicly shame him, compare him unfavorably to more exemplary passagees, reverse his passage, or rely on any of a number of other tactics. Precisely because the solo passage is occurring within a collective context, some or all of the cohorts may also be implicated in agents' tactics, the most extreme example epitomized by a decision not to promote an entire class unless one among them will report who stole a copy of the final examination from the teacher's desk and presumably intended to use it during the examination.

Because such examples suggest agents can be harsh, we need to remember that from the agents' standpoint, deviant individuals may also require protection and aid. Thus, under structural conditions where dropouts are believed undesirable, a faculty will work hard to help the slow student. A faculty will also stretch its concept of shape and allow him to move through transitional steps as if he had performed normally and even allow him to graduate (as graduate facilities have long done for students from underdeveloped countries). Where faltering or under-par performance is anticipated — as with black college students today — special arrangements may be instituted to prevent dropout, failure, or unduly slow passage. Under these benign conditions graduation can be delayed if too much damage can be done either to the reputation of the agents' organization or to others during the passagee's next passage. An example that involves organizational reputation is the delay imposed on a graduate student in receiving his degree until he has done extra reading or research. How agents look forward to the next passage is exemplified by medical faculties that frequently require exceptionally poor students to take internships under their own direction, in order that their educations be made more complete and "the public protected" as far as possible.[4] Ultimate protection of future patients would require the student be flunked out of school, but this is rarely, if ever, done so late in a student's career because his medical education is so expensive and its costs borne so largely by the state, just as the student from an underdeveloped country is carried because, however poor a student, his education is worth something to his country.

When passages are relatively loosely structured and the signs of progress more difficult to read, the agents may blame themselves for not having realized earlier that a passagee should have been dropped; but to dismiss him now would be manifestly unfair, even immoral. Graduate departments in less rigorously structured disciplines repeatedly face this problem. The more the organization cannot afford to drop deviants (at any phase of their passage), the more will it devise

4. Field notes done for *Boys in White.*

institutional means to check on the progress of its passagees. Under conditions where too many recruits have been forced on the organization, or where it over-recruits deliberately, standardized barriers to "real candidacy," as exemplified in graduate departments of large state universities, are erected. A characteristic consequence is that passagees work assiduously or frantically to pass through the barrier, knowing full well that this is the major transitional point in their passage. This is the moment of truth! Another characteristic consequence is that they are forced to juggle this priority against other priorities, so they become less expert at, or less knowledgeable about, other aspects of their education that the faculty also believes desirable. Faculties may not know this, or may know it very well but choose to run the risk of that potential consequence. In effect, the faculty's ideas of shape, which include these other matters, get disregarded or slighted.

A major problem in the agents' management of individual deviance, is that a passagee may be successful in concealing from them his departure from the desired collective shape. Continuing with the example of graduate students: one of the authors of this book once was partially discovered in his own deviance by a professor, who found him three weeks before the examination for doctoral candidacy, carefully studying the previous examination questions given by this same professor. This was the only studying that the student did for the section of the exam for which the professor was responsible. This partial uncovering of what should have been more diplomatically concealed might have prejudiced chances of passing the exam if the professor had felt more aggrieved (he reproached the student), but those chances probably would have been further decreased had the professor known the extent of the student's transgression in choosing to pass, on the basis of perusing previous examinations, without bothering even to study for this next one.

One final point about the agents' management of deviant acts and passagees: insofar as the agents themselves are a diverse lot, either exemplifying their differences implicitly in their words and acts or openly disagreeing with one another, individual passagees can model themselves after different agents. If the organization is so structured that agents with different views perform quite different organizational functions, passagees have an increased opportunity simply to choose

from different models different aspects to imitate or incorporate genuinely into their inner selves. A striking instance occurs in the education of medical residents and interns[5] who learn different aspects of
their work from very different sources, including nurses and residents,
and also come into contact with a multiplicity of older physicians
from whom they learn different things, but tend not to model their
own work and styles on any single physician. In such situations, the
final judgments of individuals are affected in no small measure by
conversation with other individuals who are going through the same
collective passage. In such passages, however, the passagee cannot
easily be censured for great deviance; because the collective passage
is loosely defined, variations in individual passage are viewed with
tolerance, and models for such passages are so diverse.

Returning once more to the agent group: a third crucially important issue with which they must cope derives from their *simultaneously putting two or more cohorts through the same passage, but each
at a different stage of this passage.* (Two or more cohorts may be going
through completely different passages, but that is another phenomenon.) Because passagees are at different "levels," as in a public school,
the organization must manage its affairs so that the passage of each
cohort will not be adversely affected (or to the least degree possible)
by the presence of other cohorts.

Under certain conditions this task involves considerable juggling
of organizational resources as well as shrewd tactics for minimizing
either friction among the "classes" or undue cooperation among
them, both of which result in agential loss of control over the passage
of one or more cohort. Some of the tactics for minimizing communication among cohorts are much like minimizing communication within
a single cohort. Sometimes a consequence of utilizing space and resources in certain ways — wittingly or unwittingly — makes contact
among cohorts quite difficult. Collegiate schools of nursing unwittingly segregate their classes in this fashion, so that while the cohesion
of individual cohorts is great the cohesion or contact among different
cohorts is minimal. Nevertheless, there is a certain amount of juggling
of resources, principally staff and time, that the faculty must manage.

Under other structural conditions, although members of different

5. Blanche Geer *et al,* "Learning the Ropes", in Erwin Deutscher (Ed.) *Among the
Poor* (New York: Basic Books, 1968), pp. 209-35.

cohorts are in intimate contact, the agent groups need not especially juggle the consequences of that contact. Undergraduate bodies, whose members meet after the freshmen year in classrooms and before then in fraternity houses and other social settings, present no special problems to faculty in so mingling. Indeed, because the solo passages are as important to faculty as the collective one, ideally if not always actually, faculty may look on this contact among classes as speeding the progress of younger students and of no great harm to older students. Compare this situation with what occurs in public schools, when young children imitate the behavior of older ones, thus speeding up their passages in what teachers (and parents) may deem inappropriate haste. We are all familiar with some of the tactics whereby elders attempt to handle this kind of unseemly phasing, as well as the important role of closed awareness in the children's management of their secret handling of their own phasing.

While discussing how and to what extent the agent groups juggle multiple cohorts, it is especially interesting to examine briefly the curious situation that obtains when the collective passage is so new that only one cohort is in passage. Aside from all the problems attendent in discovering and allowing to emerge the shape of the new passage, one important variable that affects the emergent shape, and so the fates of current passagees, is that they constitute only the "first class." The agent group also has its eye on the imagined next class. Agents who partly fail with the first class may understand that this failure will necessitate changing their modes of operation with the second class as well as possibly necessitating maximal segregation of each class from the other. Moreover, the first class can easily believe that because the program is so new, the agents do not know entirely what they are doing, and so they more openly and successfully strive for control over aspects of their collective and individual passages. Under especially stressful conditions, however, some or all may come to believe that they are guinea pigs for future classes, forgetting that they (usually) voluntarily chose to make passage under these very agents. If pressed into a clearly undesirable passage, or an undesirable transition step, the first class can even more easily believe that agents will never again act so harshly because its inexperience now leads them to be more afraid of losing control than later when it is more sure of itself.

Collective-Aggregate

Contrasted to the general structural situation where agent and passagee groups are found in organizational or institutional contexts, there is another structural situation where the *agent group functions as a collectivity but its passagees flow through its hands as an aggregate of individuals.* Aggregates can consist of a number of different individuals whose passages are managed either simultaneously or successively (or both) by the agent group. Thus, citizens who apply for and take the state's standard test for their drivers' licenses are members of aggregates who simultaneously as well as serially are in passage from non-licensed to licensed status. Each individual may regard himself as a single individual who will pass or fail, depending on his own performance. Nevertheless, for analytic purposes, we shall treat all such situations principally as aggregate passages, and only secondarily as solo passages or — insofar as individuals in the aggregate communicate with each other — as collective passages.

When conditions for these aggregate passages obtain, both *agents and passagees face respective contingent problems.* The agent group must exert control over the shape of the total aggregate passage, that is, all the individual passages totalled into a single aggregate. The agent group is also concerned with the shape of each solo passage, especially insofar as each may deviate from the norm for the total aggregate. Deviances may be upsetting in their own right, causing organizational emergencies; but they may also cause organizational crises: challenging some measure of the organization's control over the total aggregate passage. *The corresponding problem of the individual is principally to secure some measure of control over his own solo passage,* using the advantages of or getting around the disadvantages of his being part of an aggregate.

Like the collective passages, these aggregate ones occur within organizational settings. A principal difference between them, however, is that *each agent is likely to be assigned a different collection of passagees.* Each shepherds these individuals through passage, calling on institutional machinery and even on the assistance of fellow agents at various phases of a passage. Or an agent may handle some phase of a solo passage and then hand on the passagee to another agent for the next phase of the passage. A medical clinic is a good example of an organization set up to handle an aggregate of individual patients who flow through the hands of successive agents and their assistants, themselves coordinated in a fairly elaborate division of labor. An insurance company which processes auto damage claims is another example of an organization that manages aggregates.

The principal problem for a new organization is the necessity to discover, institute, and maintain the proper shape of aggregate passage. This means careful attention must be paid to the quantity and quality of passagees when they are accepted into, or chosen for, passage. Quantity is important because too many or few can create havoc with the organization's monetary or manpower resources. Recruiting the wrong passagees can also create grave problems: they might require too much effort to teach or control, or they might get discouraged and drop out of passage thus wasting the organization's time, money, and effort. But selection is only one problem; other aspects of shape necessarily must be debated within a new organization as the agents explore their own capabilities in interaction with the flow of passagees.

Review of past organizational performance is transformed into changes of policies that pertain to the shape of aggregate passage. On the basis of "our current experience," should we drop more quickly the passagees who fail or who move too slowly in passage? Indeed, should we alter the criteria by which we judge failure? Should we speed up some phases of passage, even omit some phases? Now that we have more experienced agents or can afford more of them, can we also afford to take on harder cases on whom we must expect to spend more time and effort? Can we now take on more passagees simultaneously? Can we make our division of labor more efficient, with specific personnel for different phases of passage, rather than making each agent and his assistants responsible for the totality of each individual's passage? These kinds of queries pertain not so much to solo passages as to the management of the total aggregate.

Under some conditions, agents may be allowed relative autonomy in their management of their assigned segments of the aggregate. It is easy to see the kind of conditions that mitigate against agent autonomy: when the organization is new and everyone is concerned with proper aggregate shape or when coordination of the whole enterprise itself is precarious; when agents are responsible only for certain phases of each individual performance so that articulation of phases is a necessity; when there are visibly untoward consequences to the organization of poor agent performance, including passagees' complaints or an emergency caused by agents' ineptness; when the entire organization is judged, or believes it is judged, by important other organizations in accordance with "the results" (its passagees, as products either in passage or afterward). A listing of those conditions is enough to suggest how and why organizations may run through cycles of tightening or loosening the autonomy of one or all of its agents. A single case of murder by a parolee, for instance, can cause an entire state system of parole to decrease the autonomy, at least temporarily, of its parole officers — although some of the officers may choose to resist, concealing certain of their operations from their chiefs.[6] Yet large insurance companies dealing with auto claims satisfy the conditions whereby agents' autonomy is quite great.[7]

Both the multiplicity of agents and the conditions that allow relative autonomy of agents also make possible a range of variations or latitude in the passages of individual passagees. We should not suppose that just because an organization processes an aggregate that it does so in rigid, cookie-cutter fashion. Indeed, different agents might differently decide about most matters of passage if faced with exactly the same passagee. (The organization may, of course, by choice manage a number of different kinds of aggregate passage.) Agents may also decide to make secret bargains with certain passagees, during certain of their phases keeping matters concealed from colleagues, running slight or considerable risks that this concealed latitude will cause some organizational disturbance. It may also suit the personal purposes of the agent to make these arrangements. He may believe that he will be more successful with a particular passagee if he handles him this way (allowing a parolee to live "for stability" with a woman) or he has a conscience about driving too hard a bargain in his transaction with the claimant of auto damages. Or the arrangement may save the agent extra work. It may even suit the nonorganizational purposes of the agent: he saves himself time so that he can moonlight on organizational time. However, the agent learns some

6. E. Studt's study of Parolees, Parole Agents, and the Parole System, Center for Law and Society, University of California, Berkeley.

7. H. Laurence Ross, *Settled Out of Court* (Chicago: Aldine Publishing Co., 1970).

general organizational rules that are likely to obtain — for example, the insurance company prefers not to waste time on small claims but would rather pay out first — and so tends to follow those rules in many cases.[8]

The more experienced the passagee, especially the more repeated passages he has had in this or similar organizations, the more he may be able to take advantage of what he has learned from this "system" or ones like it. He either finds his way around aspects of the system — doing well despite them — or cashes in on effective aspects of the system. The savvy automobile driver who, having moved to a new state must take the test given to new residents, may (as did one of the authors) show up at the licensing bureau within minutes before closing time, anticipating a perfunctory test by an agent, already prepared to depart for home, after the agent has assessed him on his own say-so as an experienced driver. Likewise, while inexperienced patients in large medical clinics cannot get much control over their individual treatments, patients who have repeatedly been through the organizational machinery may learn how to bend it to their purposes — taking shortcuts, cutting down on waiting time, getting the doctor whom they want while avoiding others. Clever or knowledgable passagees can even shorten or omit undesirable transitional phases, or block their involuntary passages through a totally undesirable passage. An example in the intricacies of tactic and counter tactic is the well known phenomenon of malingering by men about to be drafted into armies. If the agents who put a draftee through the initial steps of induction are not unduly suspicious of him, the malingerer may succeed by using any of a number of standard dodges. However, if the suspicion of agents is aroused, they may utilize any of a number of equally standard counter tactics. Tactically, the game is essentially identical with what occurs when a man is suspected of being a spy, except that the malingerer has no organization that stands behind him, having instructed him in tactics; and the spy is not trying to block an undesirable passage. In 1970, of course, men who prefer to delay or avoid the draft have instituted machinery, or collective generational wisdom, on which they can draw.

An entire organization can actually be different from its appear-

8. *Ibid.*

ance to its aggregate of passagees. Its agents' tactics then derive from this false identity. Thus, a con mob may pass itself off to a series of unsuspecting marks as an honest organization devoted to lucrative, albeit perhaps illegitimate, betting.[9] The mark is induced to spend his money, sometimes also illegitimately obtained and then shaken loose, after he is shaken down. If possible, the true identity of the mob is not revealed to the mark. In one famous instance when the mob did not manage to cool out a mark without his getting suspicious, the irate victim pursued the mob with such vindictiveness that eventually he got some of its members behind bars. To do this, he needed to use the counter tactic of persuading policemen to pass as innocent marks so that, being fleeced, they obtained evidence of the mob's real activity.

Even in as small an organization as a con mob (and one which manages aggregate members successively rather than simultaneously), it is notable how crucial is the articulation of this illegitimate organization's division of labor. Let one agent slip with regard to any phase of the mark's passage, and there may be an organizational emergency or even a crisis created (emergency in that the mob may lose a customer; crisis in that he may then suspect who they are and bring in the police.)

Emergencies and crises are features of aggregate passages in all organizations. An emergency is caused by some occurrence in a solo passage that runs so counter to the expected (normal) that organizational routine becomes quite disrupted . One instance is an unexpected actual or near death by a woman in childbirth. If emergencies of a given type occur frequently enough, the organization will devise emergency procedures so that in effect these events no longer cause more than minimal disruption. The violent behavior of mental patients on closed wards of psychiatric hospitals is handled with standard procedures: the patient is locked in his room, and quick-acting drugs are administered.[10]

Simultaneous or unexpected passage of members of an aggregate may produce difficult organizational situations, due to failures in resources or in articulation of agents' work. In a hospital there may

9. Edwin Sutherland, *The Professional Thief* (Chicago: University of Chicago, 1937).

10. For a discussion of emergencies, see A. Strauss *et al, Psychiatric Ideologies and Institutions* (New York: The Free Press, 1962).

be no emergency if a patient expectedly has a heart attack; the staff is prepared and can quickly begin resuscitation using appropriate procedures and necessary equipment. If three patients simultaneously have attacks, however, there may be neither sufficient manpower nor enough machines to save all three patients. If a patient develops an attack unexpectedly, the emergency procedures may not be utilized because everyone is so surprised that the institutional activity necessary to save him breaks down: staff members do not act quickly or efficiently enough, and the necessary equipment is nowhere in sight. In the aftermath of losing such patients, however, feelings of professional negligence and lessened staff morale are unlikely because the staff can realistically say, "What could we do?" They must be able to feel and answer, "Nothing."[11]

Some emergencies may be caused by passagees' attempts to gain control over their own passages, for example, mental patients' running away from the hospital or attempting suicide.[12] Other emergencies may be precipitated by agents' errors, providing the errors are discovered or are obvious enough to be understood as errors by the passagee. Even if the latter misunderstands, believing an error occurred where none did, he may cause an emergency by complaining directly to the agent or going to higher authorities. The agent may also deliberately act illegally — as in the Berkeley mass arrests of May 1969 — and seek retribution in the courts.

Emergencies develop into true organizational crises if they pose a serious threat to some of the organization's modes of operation. A crisis would occur in an organization if an ex-patient brought a malpractice suit against a hospital and a scandal ensued (the blunder was dramatically terrible or the patient was a famous public figure). Ordinarily a patient who escapes from a psychiatric hospital represents only an emergency, with staff and perhaps police mobilized to find him, but if the escapee commits a murder a genuine organizational crisis may develop against which no amount of previous manuevers (building up good will in the neighborhood around the hospital or among newspaper reporters) will prevail. Organizational crises are such drastic events that no matter how much ill feeling exists among agents, they

11. Barney G. Glaser and Anselm L. Strauss, *Awareness of Dying* (Chicago: Aldine Publishing Company, 1965).
12. Ibid.

are unlikely to precipitate an organizational crisis by allowing others' errors or negligence to reach passagees. These remain organizational secrets.[13]

An important property of aggregates is that under certain conditions they may become collectivities. This possibility is enhanced both by the fact that the aggregate as a whole is handled by an agent group rather than by single agents and by the necessity for the aggregate to appear often at organizational locales. If the aggregate members are processed simultaneously, the probability of communication among them is increased, if only because they are more likely to see each other, sit or stand near each other, and spend more or less time in one another's presence. In institutions such as medical clinics, however, a person may rarely or infrequently meet exactly the same other passagees every time he visits the clinic; in such instances information relevant to control of solo passages may be passed from one individual to another, but group solidarity will scarcely develop. In some TB clinics, however, where week after week the same patients come for strep shots, they may develop into more of a grouping and even act occasionally in common such as in making a shared complaint to the staff. In a business school described in Geer, *et al.,* [14] the student body is essentially an aggregate, each student pursuing his own learning and relating directly to the instructor, with a minimum of interaction among the students. In this kind of setting, although the students do not have much time to spend with each other and all are at different stages in their learning, a certain amount of communication occurs among them, mainly about how to handle the work or the instructor and about vital specifics such as the scheduling of the lessons. In contrast, at barber colleges (Geer),[15] where the aggregate of students is very much on its own, the students are constrained to learn mainly from one another. Compared with medical or nursing schools, however, only a minimum of student culture develops at the barber college because the aggregate never evolves into much of a collectivity (student body or class). Night schools, extension classes at universities,

13. For a discussion of secrets, see E. C. Hughes, *Men and Their Work* (New York: The Free Press, 1958).
14. Blanche Geer *et al, op. cit.*
15. *Ibid.*

and city colleges frequently have minimal student cultures for precisely the same reasons.

It is easy to see that if aggregates were too ready to evolve into active groups, they could cause organizational havoc, making demands or urgent requests that, if effected, would *radically alter the normal shape of aggregate passage.* Fortunately for organizations, aggregates only become strong collectivities under the kinds of conditions touched on earlier, so that an organization tends to face such emergencies or crises probably with less frequency than those due to other sets of conditions. (Insured persons who feel aggrieved by insufficient service from their company of choice cannot easily band together to affect organizational change; they can only drop their insurance with the company or complain individually.) It is not unknown for inept or inexperienced agents to take exactly the steps that turn an ordinary aggregate at least temporarily into an aroused grouping, even laying the basis for more persistent collectivities. The actions of authorities of institutions actually or supposedly servicing ghetto residents might be cited as an instance of this phenomenon.

In general, however, organizations which deal mainly with aggregates are discomforted and imperiled far more by their own organizational ineptness in managing aggregate shape or by the evolution of complexities — including internal schisms — that render management increasingly difficult than by their aggregates' becoming transformed into collectivities. When they do, not only the tactics of agents must change, but the organization itself must change. The rise of black student organizations in universities is a dramatic case in point.

SOLO AGENT, AGGREGATE PASSAGEES

The major contingent issues associated with this classic relationship — solo agent and aggregate passagees — derives from this fact: *each passagee usually considers himself in solo passage,* (and often voluntarily selects his agent,) *while actually the agent is juggling an aggregate of passagees.*

Here is an anecdote that will bring out important features of these contingent issues. A shrewd and unscrupulous dealer in automobiles managed his aggregate of lower-class Negro clients to cheat them of considerable money without most of his customers' being aware of this shrewd practice. If a purchaser discovered that he had been cheated, he was quite powerless to institute any retribution. When many purchasers, however, began to complain about their individual cases to a Legal Aid Society newly established to help the poor, its lawyers eventually perceived a common pattern in the dealer's operations. They filed suit against him, in the name of one of their clients.[16] This case can usefully be analyzed as follows. An unscrupulous agent handled his aggregate to maximize both his control and personal advantage. He attempted to keep a closed awareness context with individuals and, as far as possible, with the entire aggregate. When individuals began to compare notes the awareness context became more generally open, but the aggregate and individuals were still relatively powerless either to affect their own passages or those of future passagees. The best they could do was to dissuade friends from following the same (voluntary) path. When the aggregate found a strategic ally, one who knew how to use the resources of the law, the dealer lost at least partial control over his management of the aggregate's shape.

More usually, agents are honest and more or less open in handling many aspects of aggregate passage. Ordinarily, also, the passagee understands perfectly well that his agent (lawyer, physician, housing contractor) has other "clients" — sometimes a great many others. *The great problem of the agent, understandably, is that he has to juggle the competing demands made by his clients.* For instance, a housing contractor must balance considerations of time, money, and resources when deciding whether to take one more customer or whether he can finish one phase of building a house for someone while entering other phases of building with other customers. He must keep each customer satisfied enough — and inevitably many of them a bit dissatisfied — so they will not abandon him and go to another contractor or blacken his reputation to future potential customers.[17] Physicians do not face quite the same shortage of materials and assisting manpower as do the housing contractors; nevertheless, they have comparable problems in juggling the demands of clients. "Time" is in shortest supply for the physician, so he makes his patients waste or use their time rather than his own. The consequence is a lineup in his

16. We are indebted to Jerome Carlin, head of the San Francisco Legal Aid Society, for this case.

17. Barney G. Glaser, *The Patsy and the Subcontractor* (in ms.).

waiting room or the less visible lineup of his hospital patients fretfully awaiting his visit.

If a passagee clearly understands that he competes with others in the agent's aggregate or feels that his own time, money, or "case" is important enough to warrant actively countering that competition, he needs to engage in counter tactics. He may try bribing, threatening, or harassing his housing contractor. He may grumble at his physician, even hint that he may take his medical business elsewhere. He may use less open tactics, also, such as arranging to visit his physician at the very end of office hours, guessing that then the competition will have fallen off and his own precious time thus conserved. He may try to get a faster or better service from his architect or his lawyer by making himself likable, or by bringing pressure and influence to bear to get himself defined as a client who is much more important than most others.

Customers and clients also may attempt to control aspects of their solo passages by indirectly taking their competitors into advantageous account. Specialists in any field are chosen principally because they have had valuable experience with "others like me." The passagee reasons: if successful with similar cases, the specialist is good enough to handle my case. Precisely because of this indicator of success, the passagee may be quite willing to suffer the direct competition of other clients. Examples that spring to mind are those patients who wait many weeks to see, and be accepted as a client of, a respected specialist whether he is an architect, lawyer, house designer, or physician. When the agent is especially famous, a prospective passagee is willing to wait longer and put up with additional disadvantages accompanying the passage, such as the agent's idiosyncrasies, aggressiveness, or unsatisfactory scheduling of some aspects of the passage. An excellent instance is the treatment some clients of Frank Lloyd Wright suffered to get their houses built by this seemingly often willful genius.

The above examples also illustrate how the relationships are based squarely on selection of the agent by the passagee, combined with the agent's acceptance of the passagee. This *mutual voluntariness* tends to give the agent additional control over the passagee, but only under certain conditions does the agent gain the extra authority yielded to the chosen. Thus, he will have this extra authority if he can establish trust in himself or if he allows the passagee some say about technically unimportant aspects of the passage. The agent gains control also if the client has few other options: the latter has an emergency or there are no other agents easily available. (Typically the abortionist and many of his clients stand in this relationship.) The agent gains extra control also if the other options open to the client are less desirable, as when a patient is told he has TB by an examining physician, and then must settle either for treatment by this physician or be turned over to the less desirable ministrations of the public health system.[18]

However, the passagee may have room to *bargain* about features of his passage. He bargains from at least two positions of strength. The first is that usually he can withdraw from his contract with the agent. Of course, this he cannot always do without some cost to himself, as when he fires his architect half-way through the building of a house. His second position of potential strength is that he often can turn to another agent, because the latter rarely operates in a completely noncompetitive field. The effectiveness of threats to leave an agent's aegis depend, however, on other conditions which affect the agent, such as how urgent are his financial or psychological needs for the business of his passagee. A striking example: candidates at some psychoanalytic institutes are required to present two or three cases as these develop over time; so, if one of their special patients drops out of analysis, the young analyst loses valuable time in gaining his coveted certificate. Thus the intertwining of the separate passages of agent and client can be crucial for the latter's position of strength. When the agent's own passages are not harmed by potential loss of a client, the latter's threats to leave are ineffective.

There is also a species of *silent control,* of which the agent may be entirely unaware, whereby the passagee gains command over aspects of his passagee. This situation is facilitated when for long periods of time he is away from the agent's vigilant eye and especially when the agent cannot discern departures from the planned passage. As suggested by our earlier examples, patients with chronic diseases almost always depart in some measure, at some time or other from the regimens ordered by their doctors, and they may do this with great impunity if there is good likelihood that their transgressions will never

18. Walter Klick, "Problems of Regimen Compliance in Tuberculosis Treatment " (Unpublished Ph.D. thesis, New York: Columbia University, 1969).

be known. (In one instance, a diabetic woman, interviewed after repeated visits to a clinic, admitted that in order not to grow fat — she had been warned repeatedly against this — she starved herself every other day to cancel out the "tasting of foods," which she did on alternate days, as she was cooking for the family.)[19]

Compromise with an agent — a type of bargaining — can be reached through the use of *consultants*. The passagee may use them to check on his agent's judgment or to increase his own bargaining power; however, sometimes the agent may urge their use to regain lagging trust in himself or to lessen his client's resistance to next phases of a passage. The use of consultants means, of course, that the agent no longer acts purely as a solo agent; but except with very routine passages, an agent rarely operates completely independently of some kind of consultation — often unknown to the passagee — drawing on the opinions and counsel of his colleagues. He may even get that counsel without colleagues' awareness that they are giving it, if the agent astutely keeps that awareness context closed also. In a larger sense, the agent rarely operates completely alone, because he draws on the resources of his wider occupational world. Even marginal agents such as abortionists, many of whom are physicians, are serviced by the drugs and equipment common to the medical world.

Most of the passages discussed above were chosen by passagees and are desirable (except those when a passagee wants a passage reversed or blocked, as when he goes in emergency to a lawyer or physician). Probably most solo aggregate passages are voluntary and desirable. When they are not, the passage is likely either to be kept concealed, at least temporarily, from the passagee (as when an individual con foils a mark, or a burglar steals from an empty apartment), or the passagee is confronted by agential force (armed robbers). If the passagee (*e.g.* a cheated purchaser) never knows the true nature of his passage, he cannot reverse the passage via retribution; nor can he obtain retribution if he does not recognize the exact agent who put him through undesirable passage. Retribution usually involves abandonment of the solo-passagee role, and bringing in collective agencies such as the police or the law. Under some conditions the aggrieved

19. The interviewer was Shizu Fagerhaugh, on a study directed by A. Strauss.

party can act as his own agent, as when he threatens the con with a beating unless he gets his money back.

Some undesirable and involuntary passages are accomplished neither by concealment nor direct force, but by the threat of an alternative passage that seems more undesirable. Successful blackmailers use this tactic to implement their aims with successive victims. Blackmailers fail principally when they imagine the alternative to blackmail to be more undesirable to the intended victim than it actually is. And, of course, threats of blackmail are ineffective against people who have nothing to lose by exposure; such people do not become victims. Someone threatened by blackmail may choose to counter the threats by flight or by destroying the blackmailer. Blackmail among persons known to each other can also be countered if the intended victim has the necessary information similarly to blackmail his enemy.

Solo Passage

A passagee can be his *own agent* and there can be, in a sense, no other agents — or if there are, they are subsidiary to his own activity. A well known instance of the first is the phenomenon of "passing." Negroes who choose to pass in the white world may elect to do so quite by their own efforts. On occasion, however, they may have to depend on the silence of others who recognize their passing, or in special circumstances may enlist their assistance in passing at specific locales. The use of a supplementary agent is illustrated nicely by the necessity for a white journalist to get the assistance of his physician who gave him drugs for turning his skin dark, but once that was done the journalist needed nobody to pass successfully as black.[20]

In such instances of passing, it is possible to regard the unsuspecting fooled persons as an aggregate, all of whom have been made into a kind of "mark." That view of the phenomenon makes sense insofar as any one of the aggregate may threaten or actually carry out exposure of the man who is passing, thus — analytically speaking — reversing their own undesirable passage. Some possibility of error that will give away the false identity of the passing person always exists also.

20. John Griffin, *Black Like Me* (Boston: Houghton Mifflin, 1960).

Such instances of passing among a diffuse aggregate population are quite different than, say, when an immigrant slips unbeknownst into a country and passing as one of its citizens, his passage complete with falsified name and biography. Arrayed against him then, no matter how unsuccessfully, are the governmental resources of his newly assumed country.

Every independent entrepreneur is, to a large degree, reorganizing some important status passage, with all agents to that passage playing truly *subsidiary roles.* The passagee may need teachers during initial phases of his passage, and from time to time he may seek consultants, and may delegate to assistants certain agential responsibilities — but all these people are subordinate to his purposes. Even submission of oneself to some undesirable passage — such as becoming mistress to a Broadway producer — may only be a means of using an agent as a stepping stone upwards.

Such calculated use of agents during transitional phases of the total passage may take place on organizational locales, on the terrains of solo agents, or indeed may involve any of the combinations of agent and passagee discussed earlier. During these status passages, the passagee characteristically discovers new phases and aspects of his passage, and correspondingly must discover which subsidiary agents can be useful and for what purposes. One of his greatest dangers is using an inappropriate agent, or hanging on to one who has outlived his usefulness. Choice of an incompetent music teacher has ruined many a gifted, ambitious young pianist; and too great a loyalty to a teacher, for too long, has held back or ruined other careers.

Another characteristic feature of entrepreneurial passages is the *crucial discovery that actually one can guide his own passage,* rather than handing its guidance over to agents — a discovery that, if it is not just assumed, must be made in order that embarkation on the self-managed passage can even begin. All men fail to discover that they have talents that would enable them to manage certain desirable passages themselves, rather than assigning that control to specialist agents. Adherence to ideology, too, may blind them to entreprenurial possibilities: they think amateurs like themselves cannot be agents, or will not attempt the passage because ideological considerations make it undesirable.

7. MULTIPLE STATUS PASSAGES

THE ANALYSIS in this book has been based on the assumption, not yet noted explicitly, that people go through more than one status passage at a time. This multiplicity of passages sets problems based on different kinds of relationships between them. Although some status passages may be relatively *independent* of each other, others may *compete* for time and energy, often causing considerable personal strain. Multiplicity of passages may, however, help to ease the passagee's life, providing that at least one passage *supports* or helps the other. Multiplicity inevitably also sets problems of *priority:* which of various passages are of varying importance, and how does one decide on relative rankings of the passages? Given these phenomena of priority, support, competition and interdependence, a major analytic issue is their articulation by the passagee and his agents: how and to what degree, and with what consequences, are these multiple passages kept articulated?

In some societies and social groups (traditional societies and sectarian groups), many if not most of an individual's status passages are articulated through institutional arrangements: very little personal juggling or balancing of passages is required. Many ethnographic monographs illustrate the typically effective articulation of passages: the institutional control over interdependence of and mutually supportive passages, the scheduled temporal phasings, and the regulated shifts of priorities over the individual's life cycle. Even emergencies — the personally unexpected occurrences during passage, such as illness or injury or unanticipated dying — are maximally managed in accordance with institutionalized rules and arrangements. In industrialized societies, the burden is often on individuals to articulate their own passages, nevertheless, they often can rely on institutional or group arrangements — at the very least, on general social values or expectations or rationales — to support their efforts at articulation.

For instance, a man conventionally may make the passage into marriage simultaneously with entering the world of paid work, both his salary and social sanctions supporting that sequence. Or nowadays he may be able to rely on parental support to make the first passage without social censure before beginning the second. Or pressured by his girl friend who wishes an early marriage, he may reasonably refuse until he has amassed sufficient money or feels sufficiently over the initial hazards of his business career. At the other extreme, teenagers who wish to marry young may actually seek the counsel of other persons, or be convinced to wait by "reasonable" talk, or finally prevented by legal constraint.

Despite these societal instrumentalities, individuals in at least the advanced sectors of industrialized societies do confront the necessity of juggling most of their own passages. This requires a host of decisions and also the creation of strategies and tactics, not to mention the choice of proper assisting agents. As always, these status passages are influenced by variables, such as whether the passages are voluntary or involuntary, expected or unexpected, desirable or undesirable, of short or long duration.

To conceptualize the major conditions making for relative ease or difficulty in articulating passages and the consequent effects, it is useful to think initially of these properties combined in an eight-fold table. Two or more multiple passages may vary in degree of interdependence from high to low, even to being independent of each other. (Although as passages evolve, they tend inevitably to affect each other.) Interdependence may involve a consideration of *competition, priority, and "support"* among multiple passages, which vary from mutual between any two or more passages to being in *favor* of only one passage.

Competition and Priority

A status passage may tend to be so competitive that it blots out, if only temporarily, the priority claims of other passages. The most extreme example of this phenomenon is *"the crisis."* A crisis not only takes precedence over everything, but tends to be undesirable (having a mental breakdown or being fired). A crisis is also unexpected, otherwise preparations to blunt its potential consequences would have been taken.

Crises tend to *"flood"* the lives of the passagee so that virtually all other passages may have to be temporarily "frozen" or even permanently abandoned.[1] Thus, when someone becomes severely ill, he has to stay home from work or school and may temporarily have to put aside various other pursuits such as becoming an art collector or developing a promising love affair. Such flooding may last for a considerable time. (Yet some passages may be unaffected or even be supported by a crisis; for instance, occasionally the wedding date of a very sick man is hastened by the genuine possibility that he might soon die.)

Sometimes the freezing or temporary abandonment of other passages is enforced by law, as when a man diagnosed as tubercular is sent for several months into a hospital — though he is physically quite capable of carrying on with all his other passages. Such a tubercular crisis, of course, may partly or completely block or reverse other passages; being out of commission may mean a setback in a work or school career, or the patient may lose his girl friend to unhampered rivals. Many a marriage has gone to pieces through such enforced hospitalization. (It seems almost unnecessary to add that a crisis for a passagee can create temporary havoc with the related other person's passages.)

1. Leon Festinger *et al.. When Prophecy Fails* (Minneapolis: University of Minnesota, 1956).

This example of TB hospitalization suggests also that *authorities may precipitate a crisis where none should exist,* for with some frequency the hospitalization is defined as unnecessary because the diagnosis is denied by the involuntary patient. These "deniers" cause considerable trouble to the hospital staff (who may retaliate with their own tactics) and sometimes even jump ship. Everything said about such hospitalization could also be said about what happens when some men are imprisoned or drafted into the army or pressed into sudden overseas service in wartime.

A crisis may not always initiate a new passage, but may represent a reversal (a crucial demotion in a careerist's life) or a drastic decline in an undesirable but scarcely preventable passage (a worsening chronic disease or further downward mobility of an elderly couple). Tactics then used to slow the downward passage may drastically affect other status passages, sometimes being even more potent in their competiveness than the downward passage itself. Thus, regimens for chronic disease may interfere more with time and energy needed for other endeavors than even the worsening symptoms of the disease. One tactic is to balance discomfort against regimen, taking (say) drugs until symptoms lessen but reducing or doing without drugs until the cycle starts again.[2] Tactics may also be needed to mitigate the impact of a downward passage on other passages: sufferers from some chronic disease find they lose their former friends and must give up the most energetic of their pursuits,[3] but may "compensate" by making new friends among people with a similar illness,[4] may indeed even join a society composed by and run for people like themselves.

The crisis sometimes leads to mutually supporting rather than competing passages, as when alcoholics join AA and integrate their management of alcoholism with quite new endeavors. Even reversions to a member's alcoholic habit can be integrated with new friendships and new activities, as the other members stand by the reverter through his hours of periodic trial. This AA example illustrates additionally and again that although individuals must tactically choose to join the

2. Walter Klink, *Problems of Regimen Compliance in Tuberculosis* (Unpublished Ph.D. dissertation, Columbia University, 1969).

3. Fred Davis, *Passage Through Crisis, Polio Victims and Their Families* (Indianapolis: Bobbs-Merrill, 1963).

4. Marcy Davis, *Multiple Sclerosis Patients* (Unpublished D.N.S. dissertation, University of California, San Francisco, School of Nursing, 1970).

organization, nevertheless societal resources are at hand for helping individuals articulate their competing status passages. In effect, the individual's crisis may only be an emergency for the agents who stand ready with institutionalized means to help him at this crucial point in his passage. Some of the success of AA agents — much as with religious sectarians — is that they have been through the same passage as the novice.

The chief difference between a crisis and its near relative, the emergency, is that the latter is relatively expected, hence planned for, although not preventable. A good example is the periodic flooding in the lives of accountants bent on building their practice, who must anticipate spending long hours on the accounts of their clients to the virtual exclusion of all other activities during the spring months of each year. While this may lead to strains in marital and parental relations and cause some setbacks in other passages, there is greater opportunity to develop tactics to blunt the untoward effects of annual emergency. Wives are promised vacations just before or just after the busy period. Sociability is crowded into the other months. Also, after going through the first year or two of such periodic absorption of energies, an accountant may come to more realistic terms with what he cannot sustain, and give up certain passages (hobbies) without too much regret, sometimes in favor of substitutes that are less dependent on year-round freedom or on the continual keeping up of skill or effort. The associated tactics of wives are essentially attempts to keep the pressure on so that accountant-husbands will not misschedule again or will schedule better.

Emergencies may be less predictable as to exact time, but as long as they are expectable their competition with other passages can be minimized through advanced preparation. Emergencies can also be nonperiodic but of relatively determinate duration, as when a young man embarks on a business career but first strikes an agreement with his wife that they will not engage in much outside sociability and even minimize their domestic sociability until he has climbed the first couple of steps in the business organization in which he is beginning the long climb toward "success". To be successful, this negotiation must not continue into an unexpected prolongation of the expected time period.

These examples of emergencies all illustrate how potential competition among multiple passages is minimized through having clear definition of priorities, by making certain that important others understand those priorities, in juggling time and activities, and in temporarily or permanently abandoning passages of lesser importance. Insofar as those tactics fail, strains are set up within the passagee and between him and significant partners to his competing passages. Societal resources are also at hand to be used: unemployment insurance for the unemployed, voluntary health insurance for those who want it, and — to stretch a point — TV and her family for the wife of the busy young mobile businessman.

Less dramatic than crises or emergencies are those conditions under which *individuals experience stress because they find themselves in passage — or have chosen passages — that have become very competitive.* A classic instance in the American sociological literature is the upwardly mobile person who finds the requirements and satisfactions of his world of origin increasingly in conflict with the world of his aspirations. The sociological, as well as the novelistic and biographical literature, tells us there are various outcomes to this conflict. If roots in the old world are strong enough, mobility may be abandoned, including the status passages which might accompany the upward climb. The opposite may occur when roots are not deep or the mobile aspirant can find no ready compromise with family and friends even when ready to compromise; all ties with the former life then are cut. A most drastic example of such severance is one type of extreme "passing" which is well known among American Negroes and Jews, wherein the person neither occasionally returns home in secret nor keeps his former connections surreptitiously. Passing that is in more mitigated form illustrates the range of possibilities open to people who experience this competition between staying back home and moving out. The tactics — involving actual as well as symbolic continuities with "home" — are very well known and need no description here. Some of those tactics, of course, involve keeping closed awareness from some or all of one's associates. The tactics may also support, or be supported, by others of the person's passage; for instance, he may confide in his wife who helps him "not to return," or keep the secret from his wife and keep steadily passing because he is fortified by his marriage and is not willing to give it up. The above

examples make clear that articulation involves the juggling of commitments and not merely the juggling of time or goals.

*When the shapes of two or more passages become, or are about to
become competitive, sometimes societal instrumentalities are readily
available for handling priority in favor of the more desirable passage.*[5] One passage may be averted by conventional means. Young
men avoid the draft by entering on graduate studies or *in extremis*
by going to medical school, or induction may be delayed by using
standard delaying tactics such as, during World War II, getting married. These instrumentalities also allow for scheduling of passages that
might otherwise clash, as, for instance, men may arrange with the
local draft board to finish courses of study before entering the army.
In a slightly less instrumental way, but no less "societal" for being
internalized, men may control tendencies to fall in love until they have
established themselves in careers and then move right into an active
search for a wife. Social modalities also make it easy, if personality
makes it possible, for a slowly dying person to arrange and schedule
business and domestic affairs so that they are finished properly before
he dies rather than having his crisis completely overwhelm him and
the unfinished business of his life.

However, when passages compete, a person often must go
through a period of learning, of experimenting with tactics and general strategy, before he achieves enough articulation among his passages so that he establishes priorities in order not to abandon any or
to drop only the least desirable or important among them. He learns
how to juggle time so that he can turn from one passage to another
without undue strain, because, after all, many passages require only
episodic attention and energy. Or he learns to schedule his activities
so that each passage has his temporarily uninterrupted attention. Or
he discovers that he can slow down the phasing of one without actually destroying it — or draws out its duration longer than originally
intended — while proceeding full speed ahead on another passage.

He may also face the necessity of *reordering his priorities,* allocating less importance to a given passage (with its commitments) than
to others, yet learning that he need not utterly abandon the demoted
passages. An example might be the scholarly undergraduate who,

5. David Ward and Gene Kassebaum, *Women's Prison* (Chicago: Aldine Publishing
Company, 1965).

beginning to fall in love, decides that he can still get into graduate school with less than Phi Beta Kappa marks.

This last example also suggests what, of course, frequently happens: as people's identities as well as interests change, they find they must reorder priorities — in consequence, they must juggle all over again those systems of articulation among status passages that formerly worked quite satisfactorily. This *necessity for re-articulation is continual,* although not continuous in every man's life, a necessity grounded in the precarious character both of human relationships and in personal identity so dependent on them. "Precarious" does not necessarily connote destructive or undesirable qualities. A man may even undergo a crisis that is, in the clearest sense of the term, marvelous if somewhat upsetting.[6] People do strike it rich, become successful overnight even beyond their wildest dreams. While such a happening may lead a person to abandon, or temporarily slow down or freeze, some of his passages, obviously it also opens opportunities for new and highly desirable — to him — passages. These may both depend on and enhance or support his new reputation or wealth. The new passage may also further some old passages, including the indulging of some old hobbies or, less frivolously, enabling a man now to do the work he always really wanted to do or felt himself gifted at.

Competition and Interdependence

Thus far our analysis has touched on situations where two or more passages are highly competitive (that is, there is a high degree of interdependence among passages). In general, the conditions for a *low order of competition are:* when one of the passages is not very "central" or important, when both are relatively peripheral or unimportant, or when two or more major passages are kept sharply segregated and thus each is quite manageable. Where there is, however, a *low degree of interdependence,* generally management of the competition is less difficult. The clash of commitments is less severe, there is less "flooding," and the problems of timing between or among passages are more easily managed. For instance, a businessman may get interested in and begin to collect paintings. Ordinarily he can, without

6. Orrin Klapp, *Symbolic Leaders* (Chicago: Aldine Publishing Company, 1964), see "On Becoming a Celebrity."

undue strain, juggle the competing requirements of time, energy, and finances so that this avocational and his vocational career do not run grievously afoul of one another. (Nelson Rockerfeller uses the staff resources of the Museum of Modern Art to help find some of his potential purchases.)

As this example suggests, however, these *relatively independent activities not only may become slightly and occasionally competitive, but* the collector's instinct may begin to run riot and begin to use up time, effort, and money allocated previously to the business side of life. Some collectors have solved this conflict by leaving jobs or careers to become owners of art galleries; they continue to collect and yet stay "in business." They may, however, solve the conflict between recreation and business by abandoning the hobby, or finding a less absorbing one; or by genuinely curbing urges to purchase; or by putting off further collecting with promises to themselves that they will retire early and then really begin to collect "full time." A similar conflict, perhaps closer to the experiences of most of us, is when a recreation such as chess or golf begins to take a man away from home increasingly, so that marital relationships finally — if only slightly — are affected. In our jargon, the partner to the mutual marital passage complains so bitterly that her spouse needs to juggle his competing passages with more agility or to abandon the lesser recreational one.

Avocations turned into vocations are not always easily solved, especially when they "grab" the person, yet greatly disrupt other important status passages. For instance, the art collector's fiancee might have set her face against his new vocation, so that he must choose either her or it. People who have embraced habituating drugs or become hippies, thus giving up more "normal" passages, may similarly have had to break off otherwise desirable passages[7] — or have them broken off by significant others. People who become attracted to religious or political sects, frequently discover that as their "belonging" begins to lend deeper meaning to life, it becomes essentially their chief vocation, taking precedence over other status passages. In consequence, the articulation of this major passage (into sectarianism) with other important passages becomes increasingly difficult. The more absorbing the sectarian commitment becomes, the

7. A. R. Lindesmith, *Addiction and Opiates* (Chicago: Aldine Publishing Company, 1968).

more competitive it is with others. Some are easy to abandon, but the abandonment of some (such as commitments to spouses) causes infinite distress. One solution is that wife and children also become converts; another, of course, is that families break up, perhaps to be followed by new marriages between loyal sectarians. Both solutions were noticeable among converts to the American Communist Party during the 1930s, as they are today among other prominent sects.

Similarly, Latin-American physicians who train in the United States as medical residents often decide to practice here. This decision tends to result in considerable marital tension — partly relieved by the clustering of such couples in Latin-American colonies.[8] A more serious conflict once ensued when a graduate student in biochemistry completed her work for a master's degree and prepared to transfer to another university where her fiance was to teach. He, however, did not wish her to continue with her graduate education. She broke the engagement (they were both Chinese and this was an arranged match) and returned to her own university; but she lost a full year in the process.

All the above examples are meant to illustrate how, and with what consequences, initially rather *noncompetitive status passages can become highly competitive* — a transformation usually quite unanticipated by the passagees. However, passages can remain quite noncompetitive so that very little resource is called for in juggling their small degree of interdependence. Perhaps it is necessary to add that a passage with little interdependence can eventually become quite supportive of each other, as when a man's mistress not only may not threaten but even strengthen his domestic relationships, or strengthen others which have little to do with his domesticity. This point leads to the question of how multiple passages, when properly articulated, can support rather than compete with each other.

Support Among Passages

Articulation of specific passages indeed may be necessary if *one depends on another for its initiation or continuance.* As Becker and Geer illustrate in detail, making a satisfactory "grade point average"

8. Examples taken from Rue Bucher's study of socialization.

was a necessary condition, at least at the University of Kansas, for pursuit of goals that had little relevance to getting an education, such as those attained by dating or engaging in campus politics.

In the "necessary condition passage," the signs by which someone indicates to important agents that he is making satisfactory progress are not always so unambiguous as grade points. For instance, parolees must convince their parole officers that they are making progress in various associated passages — as in the areas of work and friendship — but are not able always to have the signs read correctly; in fact, officers may read the signs incorrectly. Parolees must shrewdly assess their officers' criteria for progress in associated passages; for instance, "shacking up" may be read approvingly as a sign of stability — but it must be done with the right woman. Officers, however, will indicate the proper associated passages and their indicators, even will suggest settling down with a good woman.[9] Signs of retrogression must be concealed from agents; or, as in the instance of university students who cheat successfully, may be faked.

Whether genuine or false, and whether open or closed awareness prevails, the main point is that passages important to a passagee may depend on others who are less central; and gatekeeper agents, with reviewal and punitive power, then exist. The hierarchy of importance concerning passage usually is quite the reverse, of course, for agents. Even such an instance as woman's reluctance to marry a man until he has proven himself both a steady provider and an absolute nondrinker indicates that a vitally necessary participant in a man's important passage can raise associated passages to at least temporary importance. In effect, the participant in a really important passage functions quite like the parole agent — and probably is more difficult to fool because the conditions contributing to open awareness are more in her favor.

In working out the articulation of a necessary to a more vital passage, phasing may be of the utmost importance. *Conventional modes of scheduling abound for easing this juggling of phases.* For instance, middle class women in America now customarily plan to work for two or three years before marriage, even when engaged when they begin work, in order to save enough money to be financially

9. E. Studt's study of Parolees, Parole Agents and the Parole System, Center for Law and Society, University of Calif., Berkeley.

comfortable once they are married. The marital passage begins, in effect, even before or shortly after first employment, but actual marriage is delayed until later. Similar conventional schedules are built into the structure of institutions, so that, for instance, students are helped in juggling their necessary educational and important noneducational pursuits by the common mood and understandings that prevail around exam time and lead to a temporary slowdown of all except educational concerns. Athletic competitions are not scheduled during examination time. However, because ordinary quizzes are both less crucially important and less institutionally scheduled, they require much more individualized management by the students.

These examples illustrate problems of pacing where one passage is necessary for another. *Temporal management also may be crucial where status passages are mutually supportive* rather than where one is strictly necessary to the other. A garden variety example is that the pleasures of vacationing for some people are closely linked with the exhausting or boring qualities of work. For some, those qualities of work are made bearable both by memories of past vacations and anticipations of a forthcoming vacation. A vacation taken too early or too late can be disappointing, and if too short or too long the vacation can spoil entry back into work. By virtue of unpleasant or disappointing experience, some vacationers also learn to taper off their work as vacation time draws near, knowing that otherwise they "fall off the edge" into vacation, and so do not unwind enough to enjoy the first few days of vacation. *Such articulation of passages involves both expectation and control of potentially disrupting circumstances.*

A usually less delicate articulation of passages but equally requisite, is involved in the phenomenon of moonlighting. Here the two passages may have less interdependence, but, if interdependent, their requirements may be more competitive than supportive. Art students sometimes find that moonlighting on jobs that require artistic skills actually harms their artistic sensibilities and prefer therefore to earn money at jobs which have nothing to do with art.[10] But in the instance of social workers (described in a thesis by Bogdanoff and Glass)[11] who surreptitiously carried on lucrative ventures while supposedly doing case work, the jobs were mutually supportive and were in nice tempo-

10. From an unpublished study by Anselm Strauss.
11. University of Chicago, Department of Sociology, 1954.

ral balance. The social worker's primary problem, of course, was not so much a matter of managing time as keeping secret his illegitimate activities, initiated and carried on during the agency's time.

The mutual supportiveness of many passages flows from the very nature of men's psychological constitutions and their socializations, abetted by various institutional arrangements. For instance, as both graduate and undergraduate students know, combining their pursuit of studies with unmarried domesticity often can prove mutually supportive enterprises. Many a student has "steadied down" through the development of such domestic relations, while the educational efforts themselves lend richness to the evolving domestic passage. Appropriate tactics may be needed, of course, both to initiate such domesticity and to keep competition between it and education at minimum.

Some students may regard those two passages as impossibly competitive or "by nature" morally inappropriate. So may their parents, even though the couple favors the arrangement. If the parents can act as powerful agents of control, they can prevent or break up the arrangement by destroying one or other of the passages — pulling the offending child out of college or persuading him or her to quit the illegitimate relationship. Therefore, these control agents may need to be kept in the dark about the true state of affairs. Mutual pretense is not unknown however, especially on the part of the parents of the girl who tactfully ignore the situation.

Mutually supportive passages may grow at least temporarily competitive. Upon the birth of a first child, the parents, though previously excited together throughout the pregnancy, may find themselves in increasingly tense relationship because the mother becomes too absorbed by the requirements of ministering to the baby or becomes too engaged in loving it. The husband's reactions need to be managed properly in order that the mother can get both her passages satisfactorily articulated. Of course, he also needs to get his dual passages, the old and the new, articulated better. A study by Betty Highley[12] shows that a first pregnancy may also reactivate parental relationships, long since seemingly finished or stabilized, consequently interfering with current passages. The new mother may relive some of her stormy childhood relationships with her parents, which disturbs her

12. Unpublished manuscript, University of California Medical Center, San Francisco.

own parental and domestic passages. Ordinarily these earlier relationships either are independent of and irrelevant to the later passages or in subtle ways are supportive to them.

Mutually supportive passages can become so competitive that one may be abandoned. As is well known, the route upward to female stardom in Hollywood or on Broadway may involve sexual involvements with male directors and producers. Occasionally a romance leads to marriage, and the wife gives up her career, either because it is immediately the more desirable or the husband persuades her of its priority. Sometimes, however, she becomes his pygmalion, and her work and her marriage become even more mutually supportive than were her premarital romance and work. Supportive passages can change only mildly into immensely supportive ones. It hardly seems necessary to illustrate that point.

Less obvious, perhaps, is that as supportiveness increases one consequence may be a corresponding increase of competitiveness with still other passages, which previously were either themselves supportive or were mildly competitive. Considerable rethinking of priorities and careful articulation of the changing hierarchy of priorities is then necessary. The point can be illustrated in extreme version if we imagine coming suddenly, whether unexpectedly or not, into a sizeable amount of money. Unlike someone who gradually accumulated it, who almost unconsciously might juggle his passages as savings and income increased, the person who comes quickly into money cannot, to begin with, take his time deciding what to do with all that money. Even if he anticipated coming into money and planned what to do with it, very likely he will find his passage into wealth affecting his other passages. The new one may not quite present a fateful crisis, but aspects of the passage may have something of that quality. He has to learn how to "handle" the money, what financial agents or agencies to use, what markets in which to operate — that is, he has to initiate passages with which he is unfamiliar, especially if he came into his money suddenly. Soon he will find himself beseiged, after he begins investing, by financial agents who wish to get in on his financial business. He may discover after awhile that he had better leave one broker or banker and go to another; or learn that he had been prey to certain kinds of virtual institutionalized robbery because of his ignorance of financial matters. Even if resolutely determined not to waste time in managing his own money, certain of his previous status passages are likely to be affected. He may decide — or it may almost unwittingly happen — to begin changing his consumer styles, such as by buying a bigger house in a nicer neighborhood. That purchase may mean a gradual dropping of some friendships and initiation of newer ones with higher-status neighbors. A cooperative family also speedily will help to change his consumer tastes so that he begins, quite literally, to enter new social worlds, perhaps taking up yachting or other expensive recreations, which represent passages into new universes of discourse with special languages, activities, and participants. His problems of articulating old and new passages are only too evident.

His condition, including both its attending difficulties and challenges, only highlights what we all face with our multiple passages. Any person's "knife-edge present" (the phrase was coined by G. H. Mead) represents a temporary stasis in the flux of changing relationships among the plurality of his status passages. Everything conspires to insure that given passages will become more or less competitive, and others will become more or less supportive. In the foregoing pages we have sketched some of what goes into that "everything conspires." Attentive readers will know that a fuller, more detailed picture would necessitate a more thorough step-by-step comparative analysis, using just those kinds of variables treated throughout this and previous chapters. That analysis would also take more explicitly into account what we have left implicit; namely, that virtually everyone is implicated in other persons' passages as agents; so the relationships of their own passages are, in patterned ways, much affected by their agentships.

8. STATUS PASSAGE THEORY APPLIED: TEMPORAL ASPECTS OF SOCIAL MOBILITY

THE EXAMPLES of status passage peppered throughout the preceding chapters were meant to suggest some data on which our theory of status passage is grounded. The examples also hinted at the potential efficacy of the theory for study and analysis of a considerable range of substantive areas. To show more specifically how this formal theory might be utilized in developing a substantive theory (theory about a given substantive area),[1] we offer in this chapter a discussion of certain aspects of social mobility in America. In effect, we shall develop a partial substantive theory which bears directly on temporal aspects of mobility.

The substantive theory was formulated some months after Chapter 3 ("Temporality") of the present book was written.[2] By no means

1. See the next chapter for a discussion of the relationships between formal and substantive theory.
2. It is one of four chapters, each developed from status passage theory, that appears in Anselm Strauss, *Contexts of Social Mobility* (Chicago: Aldine Publishing Co., 1971). See Part III, Chapter 2, "Temporal Aspects of Mobility."

does the substantive theory follow, point-by-point, the formal theory. Rather, it was developed by several times rereading the chapter on the "temporality" of status passages, and then thinking carefully about already collected data which might pertain to temporal aspects of American social mobility. The product of this analysis was a potentially useful segment of substantive theory. If properly qualified and densified[3] by careful research, it would in turn add to the modification and densification of the formal theory of status passage.

In any analysis of the temporal aspects of mobility, at least three principal issues must be considered: *the amount of time* committed to achieving or preventing mobility; *the rate* of movement, whether up or down; and *the temporal articulation* of actions pertaining to mobility.

Temporal Commitment

Those who remember Budd Schulberg's *What Makes Sammy Run*[4] will easily recognize that one characteristic of this driven man was his continuous, round-the-clock, effort to "reach the top." In committing himself to that goal, Sammy simultaneously committed himself to unceasing total effort. Virtually every act was subordinate to his enterprise. All contradictory impulses or desires were sternly repressed. Even time that he spent with acquaintances or women was converted into a means for getting ahead; that is one reason why he could be read as excessively manipulative, calculating, and self-centered. If, now, we change direction downward and consider how a working-class family manages to keep its balance just above "the poverty line," we see that a similar commitment of virtually total time may be necessary. Commitment of time can range from total to negligible, and vary tremendously for different phases of climbing and falling (or standing still). Different persons who are implicated in a man's mobility may agree or disagree about the necessity for amounts of time committed. And everyone concerned may rethink decisions about temporal commitments.

Because not everyone devotes himself as wholeheartedly as Sammy or the fearful worker to striving for mobility twenty-four

3. For the notion of densification, see the next chapter.
4. Budd Schulberg, *What Makes Sammy Run* (New York: Random House, 1941).

hours a day for a lifetime — usually mobility activities are intermittent, rather than continuous, even when frequent — most mobile persons must juggle the time at their disposal, allocating various amounts of it to different kinds of activities. The classical example of juggling is the ambitious man whose mobility time is severely threatened by a demanding wife and who must steer his course between ambition and wife. This, of course, is why some men do not look for a marriage partner, or allow themselves to fall in love, until they are well up the social or business ladder — and why they try to choose wives who always will be relatively undemanding of time, or at least flexible enough to adjust their time budgets to those required by mobility.

Juggling is, of course, inextricably linked with motivation, that is, with priorities pertaining to desire and identity. American movies often show the hero caught between crossfires of motivation: should he settle for less success but have a loving wife; should he choose the less desirable but more useful (for mobility) of two women; should he leave his pinnacle of business success and descend a little so he can marry that gorgeous girl? What makes juggling a less than overwhelming problem is that most people do not expect forever to be juggling exactly the same balls, for juggling is related to expectations about phases in life. Thus a young physician can promise his wife, and himself, that after his time-consuming internship and residency he can spend more time with her and the children. He may be wrong about that expectation, but at least he acts on it. An ambitious young scientist can confidently proceed on the assumption that he must "work his ass off" until he has a secure reputation, then he can coast a little. If wives are persuaded, they will wait out the troublesome period; if not, the marriage may break up. The wife (like any party to a plan) also may disagree about the amount of time really needed to mount the mobility ladder, and if this disagreement is strong or of considerable duration it can destroy the marriage. When expectations about expenditures of future time are drastically underestimated — as they are more apt to be when the mobility route is unstandardized or if the person is relatively ignorant about the route — there may be not only consequences for domesticity, but even for health, even for the motivations that originally led to the temporal commitment.

To predict accurately the temporal commitments necessary for future phases of life, and just as accurately to foresee how one will feel about the necessary motivation during each of those phases, is a prophetic gift not given to most men. A potential hazard, therefore, for the upwardly mobile, at any level, is that they come to regret commitments made many years ago. As a 34-year-old advertising man, a resident of an upper-class Chicago suburb, said after noting that he was established:

> Do I like my job. No. I deplore it. I hate it, I come home sick at night about it. . . .Maybe I'm ready to try to make it on my own in free-lance writing. But at this point, it's irrelevant. I now have a family, two children, and I've got to weigh that balance against the other balances. . . .The trap, of course, is my past. I've been very successful writing for advertising agencies and I have a mortgage and a standard of life.[5]

Such men may however, choose to reverse some of their upward mobility. Parents face the opposite problem when trying to motivate children to spend current time that will pay off for future phases of mobility. Often the children do not understand why they must study so hard when there are so many other interesting alternative activities.

The difficulty of accurately predicting phase and motivation is compounded by an additional one: the degree to which the mobility enterprise was successful. One consequence of being much less successful than anticipated or hoped is a decision to give up striving — and spend one's time otherwise, or at least to cut down on the time expended: "There would never be the same hay in the bundle again. The ass would never have to walk after it so assiduously. . .his career was as good as over. He had gone as far as he could go."[6] People can also give up fighting for other kinds of mobility, whether trying to drop or opt out against parental wishes, say; or to prevent themselves from falling further down the ladder than they have already. Many a person after years of struggle has given up and, totally dispirited or terribly sick, slipped finally into poverty.

These junctures are points of crucial decision. In another quote from Marquand we see a man making a decision to abandon his repeated failures to rise (he did not abide by the decision, nonetheless his sentences exemplify the point about critical decisions):

> You can get so far by effort, Charley. You will find you can obtain a little

5. Studs Terkel, *Division Street: America* (New York: Pantheon Books, 1967), pp. 218-19.

6. John Marquand, *Point of No Return* (Boston: Houghton-Mifflin, 1949), p. 554.

hay but if you reach for more you'll get a sharp rap on the muzzle. . . .I know I'm right because I've tried to get some of that hay. Don't worry. It's all over now. I won't try again. All I want now is to keep out of the rain and to manufacture a suitable waterproof. I'm tired of the system, Charley. I'm delighted to give up.[7]

Of course, critical decisions — or reviews — also can eventuate in renewed efforts at mobility with corresponding greater expenditure of time.

Although someone has been successful at whatever form of mobility was elected, events may turn out so that too much success destroys his plans for "slowing down" after that success. Nowadays this is a common occurrence with businessmen who have been so successful that they can sell their businesses to larger firms for considerable profits — but only on condition that they remain as high executives with the encompassing firms; this means they actually may work harder than for several years past. Planning about later phases of life can also misfire around downward mobility; for instance, inflation cuts in on the purchasing power of people with pensions, so retired men may have to take jobs, usually paying less than the old ones, to maintain their standards of living; or they moonlight during the years just before retirement to compensate for the now expectable, drastic impact of inflationary prices. Retired college professors have resorted to both kinds of tactic.

Besides sacrificing his wife or family through keeping his "nose to the grindstone," a man may sacrifice genuine alternative opportunities to get ahead; sometimes these are better opportunities than the one he is pursuing. Again, he may not be losing much except wasted time, better spent at domestic affairs, leisure, or other pursuits. However, a young lady of working-class family, engaged to a medical student, and very much on the "make" once confessed, "I'm worried about the next couple of years. Here I'm putting all this time and feeling into this relationship with Steven, and to have it not work out, it would be terrible."[8] She may only be wasting time before she finds another middle-class boyfriend, or she may really be missing her golden opportunity because she is already twenty-four. It is even possible for someone to spend too much time at something only to get

7. *Ibid.*, p. 221.
8. Terkel, *op. cit.*, p. 20

bad marks for overwork or overcompulsiveness, or to be judged as really compensating for a lesser degree of skill; so that those who work more quickly get promoted faster or further. (The "greasy grind" is the students' equivalent of the man who doesn't necessarily win the major prizes of life.) A common and rather poignant example of too great a temporal commitment — too much as well as too long — is a man who achieves modest occupational success through some specialization, only to realize later that less time spent at more general tasks would have gotten him a higher position and more prestige. Aside from frustration at such an outcome, a man can feel locked into a job or a business organization because his very specialization — at the job or in the organization — gives him little leverage in a highly competitive job market. ("The irony of it was that after years of work one became specialized, used to the ways of just one organization, too old to start again in a new one. He had seen plenty of men his age looking for a job.")[9] This is where awareness of what kinds and amounts of effort will pay off, not only in avoiding frustrations and doleful outcomes, but — to emphasize again the expenditure of time — permits more effective set of tactics. Among the latter are the taking of shortcuts, the cutting of corners, and best of all, the utilization of effective timing (such as working hard in public although loafing in private).

Rate of Mobility

Rates of mobility vary in degree from very rapid (as in sudden ascent of a previously unknown actor to stardom) to exceedingly slow. Slow and fast rates of mobility mean both total courses of mobility and their transitional phases.

Warner and Abegglen in their research on occupational mobility in American business and industry note: "Within fifteen years of becoming self-supporting, more than half of the men studied were major executives and a quarter were minor executives."[10] Fifteen years is, nevertheless, a sizeable stretch of time; but more important

9. Marquand, *op. cit.,* p. 139. See also Terkel, *op. cit.,* p. 122. The speaker is a Mexican-American: "I've fallen into that pattern that everybody's crying about. That security. I'm forty-two years of age now. If I get fired from my job, what am I gonna do? How many first helpers do they want there in the backyard?"

10. *Occupational Mobility in American Business and Industry, 1928-1952* (Minneapolis: University of Minnesota Press, 1955).

for our immediate discussion is that the climb upward is relatively well-regulated and supervised, and that the multiple routes upward are fairly well defined. The paths of movement of personnel through the system of positions that make up the organizational structure of corporations and firms tend to be relatively stabilized. Patterns of vertical (and horizontal) movement constitute the various types of career lines that terminate at various levels of the management hierarchy. "The majority of these lines are minor and terminate at lower executive levels; others move beyond these positions and branch off into middle management; a few major lines lead to the top."[11] To make certain that competent and trained persons move into the right positions at the right time, more or less exact and differential training is provided at the various positions. In consequence, certain ones operate as critical junctures or testing points: the individual's performance determines how high he will be moved and possibly at what rate. In any event, the "speed at which individuals move along specific career lines tends to follow fairly identifiable timetables. Acceptable age ranges are identifiable for the various strata. While these age ranges are not usually defined explicitly, they nonetheless exist in terms of some of the criteria used by management in determining who moves and who does not. . . .If an individual does not move out of a given position and into another by a certain age, there will be a high probability that he will never move farther."[12] When such timetables exist, individuals are able to assess their progress fairly well. "Given a stable organization, he can frequently do this with considerable accuracy." An important ingredient of such assessment is the rehearsal of one's future through observing what has happened to other men as they have passed through the stages above oneself.

The above description pertains to mobility routes where the steps upward are relatively prescribed and also scheduled, and where that scheduling and prescription is relatively apparent to the aspirants. Of course, there are many variants of that situation; to see them, we need only change the important variables. If a company is undergoing great changes, career lines will be changing, totally or in part, so that the steps upward (or downward) become less regularized, and scheduling

11. Norman Martin and Anselm Strauss, "Patterns of Mobility Within Industrial Organizations," *Journal of Business*, Vol. 29 (1956), pp. 101-10.
12. *Ibid.*

may speed up or slow down for various phases of a career. Or new career lines will be evolving but with relatively undetermined rates and even undetermined steps. Even when the career lines are fairly stable, the signs that denote progress or "standstill" may not be altogether clear to the mobile person. Some positions, for instance, are used by management as end-points in the careers of personnel who have not made the grade, but those positions also are used to season other men expected to rise much further. It may require "considerable discernment on the part of the mobile individual to determine the category into which he falls." When horizontal movement in big companies is great, ambitious employees may fail to read accurately the meanings of their assigned geographical moves: the rate of their horizontal movement may be swift but vertical movement actually may be quite slow — or relatively frozen. Candidates may not recognize, either, that certain phases of their careers are crucial testing points while others phases are not. (Said a lawyer in a large firm, "When, after I had worked for eight years in the tax department, they asked me to change to corporation law, I did not know what to make of it, but I changed. They had an opening in this other department and were trying me out.")[13]

The amount of time spent in transitional positions may depend on unexpected happenings, such as the death or quitting of some employee at a higher position than the aspirant. The reverse can also happen: the demotion or blocking of a sponsor can affect the rate of movement of his protégé. The lack of movement of people directly above can slow up or relatively freeze one's own movement into a higher position, especially if those positions are scarce, either because the company is not expanding, or because the individual is already high up on the executive ladder where higher positions become increasingly fewer. Among the personal consequences of unexpected slowdowns or blockages are, of course, frustration, despair, and anger, but also determination to "wait it out"[14] or a decision to quit trying or to leave the company — or to bluff by threatening to leave. Firms have counter strategies: promising future promotions, increasing in-

13. E. Smigel, *The Wall Street Lawyer* (New York: The Free Press, 1965).
14. "The tension was beginning to undermine his judgement and self-control but if they wanted to keep him waiting, he was not going to show that it bothered him." Marquand, *op. cit.,* p. 80.

come but without extra status, and so on. The need for counter strategies is all the more urgent when an employee leaves with company secrets, or is lured away by a competing company that rewards him with swifter promotion.

When final blockage or even demotion (though without great loss of income or prestige) can be anticipated, a mobile person can get more psychologically set for that contingency, and even think through alternative financial or employment plans.[15] As Fred Gouldner notes, "anticipatory adaptions" are influenced by others' demotions. "(He) had thought it never could happen to him. He wasn't mentally prepared. So I said I should be. If it happens what are you going to do? So every city I go to I make sure I make some friends and nice business contacts!"[16] In large law firms, according to Smigel, blocked mobility is so expected by young aspirants, who can see how few opportunities are available for attaining a partnership, that by the eighth year only two or three of ten recruited simultaneously remain with the firm. Relatively expected demotions or blockages are adapted to in a variety of ways, rather well described in a number of sociological writings.[17] These adaptions include settling for less than was desired, usually by getting certain accompanying rewards such as buying a nice house, living in California, or shifting effort to community affairs. Business firms may help adaptations by giving actual increases of salary, occasional foreign travel assignments that are pleasurable, and best of all by considerably obscuring the actual fact of demotion or

15. "One of the most important findings in this study was that these management employees accept the real possibility of a demotion in their career. They saw demotion as a normal part of their future . . . . Witness this observation . . . : 'I like this job and realize it isn't a lifetime one and I will have to go either up or down. From what I gather in looking at assignments, you have every opportunity to peak out at 45 or 50 . . . Realistically for 99 percent it does peak out.' . . . the culture of the organization encompasses a belief in the normality, almost the inevitability, of demotion. Sixty-three percent of the executives. . .foresaw the possibility. Their attitude is best expressed by the one who reported: 'In my circumstances, you have to be stupid not to look to the future and not to have a philosophy about it. For a man to be in it and not develop a philosophy about moving up or down — he would be a nut.' " Fred H. Gouldner, "Demotion in Industrial Management," *American Sociological Review,* Vol. 30 (1965), 714-24; pp. 276-77 in B. Glaser, *Organizational Careers* (Chicago, Aldine Publishing Co., 1969).

16. F. Gouldner, *op. cit.*

17. B. Glaser, *op. cit.,* especially Part VI "Managing Demotion," pp. 263-306.

permanent blockage. Insofar as the actual situation is made apparent to others, the individual is more liable to feel publicly shamed.

By contrast, unexpected final blockage or demotion is more likely to result in difficult adaptations. Immediate reactions may include temporary withdrawal of effort, and hostility, apathy, and moroseness. Long-range reactions may include, at lower levels of management becoming anti-management in orientation and identifying downward in position, plus face-to-face relationships with employees (becoming) the chief work satisfactions. At higher levels, executives may become increasingly intractable and develop a tough, hard-boiled quality and an individualistic philosophy that makes them treasure autonomy. They may come to look upon their departments or divisions as private baliwicks and develop possessive attitudes toward them.[18] They tend not to delegate authority and so provide inadequate training for rising subordinates. Gouldner adds other consequences for all but men at the very top of management, such as increased absenteeism, moonlighting, increase in abuse of privileges, formation of power cliques and, of course, an increased turnover of employees.[19] Where an unexpected contingency is due to a power struggle, there is even more feeling of being "done out" of just desserts and more anger at the company — rather than reflection on one's own possible inadequacies. If, in addition, there has been outright betrayal by sponsors or superiors, anger will be compounded.

While demotion and freezing occur with regularity in corporate careers, certain other kinds of mobility routes probably are riskier in terms of the speed and the distance of potential catastrophic demotion. Hence, people who rise through those kinds of mobility routes must plan for those contingencies or suffer the consequences. For instance, airline pilots, through decline of their physical abilities, can quickly be washed out, losing their jobs and incomes. The same is true of musicians and baseball players. Performers whose positions are subject to such disastrous shifts typically protect themselves by investing in businesses (air pilots buy gas stations) or develop skills that are often related to their present occupations (movie stars buy businesses and sometimes also become directors or producers). As a result of contingent disasters that are not foreseen or planned for, there exist

18. Martin and Strauss, in Glaser, *op. cit.,* pp. 264-65. p. 216.
19. B. Glaser, *op. cit.,* pp. 293-94.

phenomena such as the tennis bum, the third-rate piano teacher, and the fallen movie star who ends up in grade C pictures or becomes a "voice" for TV commercials.

Unexpected but slow rises or descents (to various distances) are also possible in this not altogether predictable world. Some people are really surprised at the even modest heights to which they gradually have risen, whether by efforts of their own or through unexpected circumstances. Their reactions tend to be quite different from those of people who expected to rise or who are genuinely impatient at their slow rises. Their reactions are likely to be ones of surprised delight, almost disbelief, combined with reluctance to give up comfortable styles of living just because they have risen, sometimes also awkwardness in socializing among those whom they continue to believe are their superiors. Unexpected, slow downward mobility, from an original position, understandably has quite different consequences. These latter are evoked by the images of the formerly affluent who have drifted down to shabby gentility or the resentful white-collar workers who compare their shrinking incomes unfavorably with those of unionized skilled workers.

Those mobility outcomes stand in marked contrast, both in route and in mood, with what happens to many, if not most, lower-class urban Negro males: although they may dream of "breaking through," they know realistically most of the time that never are they going to go anywhere — except perhaps to be worse off than now. According to Carl Werthman, by the time they are twenty-five or so, "they are beaten down;"[20] they have given up trying to hit their heads against an impermeable ceiling. Their despair and apathy is quite something else than that of people whose original position has been lost through slow, almost unseen, attrition — just as their reactions are different than those of frustrated blacks who, although they may have been somewhat mobile are yet angry at their own and their race's slow mobility, and were the chief participants in the great riots of Watts, Detroit, and other cities during the late 1960s.

Swift ascents and descents — especially when unexpected — are brought about by different conditions and are likely to result in rather different sets of consequences. Horace Cayton, the Negro sociologist,

20. Personal Communication, based on research in San Francisco.

recounts in his autobiography two pertinent, revealing episodes: one about his quick ascent and another about a speedy descent.[21] Cayton was raised in a middle class family, devoted to hard work, education, and good deeds. Following the family ideals, Cayton left Oregon to pursue his graduate studies at the University of Chicago. To help support himself, he got a job at a community center. Before he quite knew it, beginning with the making of occasional speeches about race relations, he found himself in much demand as a speaker and consultant and journalist, quickly receiving acclaim as a nationally-known "race leader." That kind of speedy ascent is heady, exciting, gratifying, and more than a little bedazzling. For Cayton eventually it was also demoralizing, in some part because he became disillusioned with his role (the Negro cause was not improving) and in some part because his upbringing had helped to drive him toward personal integration with whites (including marriage with a white) rather than deep commitment to the cause of Negroes. He left his job with the community center, moved to New York where he did unsatisfying research that was not appreciated by the social welfare agency that employed him; then he became quickly demoralized, increasingly hit the bottle, and remained down and out for some months. His despair and almost total loss of self-esteem is revealed most poignantly during a description of his joining a medical line-up with other skid-row types where he sold his blood for a few necessary pennies. Although too dispirited and ashamed to maintain contact with most of his friends, it is revealing of his refusal to give up altogether that he hung on grimly to his connection with the Pittsburgh Courier, somehow turning out his weekly column for that Negro newspaper. (Eventually he was able to reverse himself upward, but that is another story.)

The consequences of sudden, unexpected, and often undreamed of great mobility are suggested by the careers of celebrities, stars, and heroes. Their quick ascents are due less to their personalities and skills — although these may be necessary conditions — as to the efficacy of promotional campaigns or the unpredictable but passionate reactions of mass audiences. As Orrin Klapp and others have noted,[22] such

21. Orrin Klapp, *Long Old Road: An Autobiography* (New York: Trident Press, 1965).

22. Orrin Klapp, *Heroes, Villains and Fools* (Englewood Cliffs, N. J.: Prentice-Hall, 1962).

celebrities have to contend with some very strange manifestations of hero-worship; and while some dote on adulation, others shrink from it and take great steps to keep their private lives untouched by their public appearances. Heroes such as Lindberg develop elaborate tactics for minimizing public display and contact. Celebrities may also have to keep their adorers ignorant of their less-than-perfect private lives, hiding (or having their agents hide) vices that are not consonant with their public images. Klapp has also commented on the occasional transformations of heroes into fools or villains, with their quick descent from positions of prominence and even influence and power.[23] The transformation is brought about either by the successful tactics of enemies or by a set of circumstances which end by defacing the hero (as when Bill Tilden was discovered to be a homosexual). If the quick, unexpected ascent, however, turns out to be a permanent rise, the mobile individual has at least one important problem: to adjust his former life-style to his new position. That is not such a simple task. To help him, there are agencies and agents who teach him or her how to dress, eat, talk, walk, as well as how and where to spend his money and his time. He may not find it easy to distinguish genuine friends and well-wishers from those who wish merely to part him from his money or to shine in his glory. Sometimes he discovers, also, that those who have inherited their positions or earned them by good, hard work and demonstration of ability will refuse to acknowledge that he has risen to their level; even a rapidly transformed style may not win him that battle. One consequence of that rejection is the formation of style-cliques of persons who have failed to storm the symbolic heights. Slow, expected ascents may end with rebuffs from the more established, but at least the aspirants have had more time to make themselves stylistically acceptable.[24] Such rebuffs may come to mobile people who rise to any level, not simply to high heights.

23. *Ibid.,* see also Orrin Klapp, *Symbolic Leaders* (Chicago: Aldine Publishing Company, 1964), esp. pp. 101-21.

24. A nice fictional instance is provided by Louis Bromfield's Mrs. Parkington, whose husband finally struck it rich in western mining, and with whom she then invaded the East. Mr. Parkington was wise enough to hire a slightly declasse French lady as a companion and stylistic coach for his wife, who would be instrumental in crashing the ranks of the less recently rich. See *Mrs. Parkington,* (New York: Harper, 1952).

Another kind of quick rise involves a decision made in favor of a quick, rather than a slow or perhaps delayed, rise. The classic example is deciding not to get more education but to go out right away and get a paying job. One potential consequence, of course, is that this haste cheats the person of chances for greater mobility. Higher paid rather than lower paid jobs can also be elected, without awareness that the race may belong to the slow but steady employee. Another variant of such choices is that of the lower income girl who in favor of an ordinary marriage chooses to strike out on her own, seeking a source of quick money for clothes and fun, and who may end up with a "better" marriage but is certainly just as likely to end up, as the saying goes, "on a downward path."[25] Similarly, the early case studies of delinquent boys published by Clifford Shaw in the 1930s,[26] reflected the choices afforded boys in the slums: whether to choose a seemingly problematic if prudent customary course (taking an ordinary job) or to engage in illegal practices that might bring quick money and immediate local prestige. The models for both mobility routes were equally visible to the boys. Decisions in favor of immediate money and prestige often led to prison and downward careers, but sometimes they paid off handsomely and over the long haul. After all there was, and is, a sustaining social structure for such illicit mobilities. There is equally a substantial structure that locks delinquents into downward or blocked mobility once they have received prison sentences. To paraphrase a very intelligent Negro parolee in the California system: I envy those who have made it either by hard work or by brainy trickery, and I would like to do the same — by either way — but there's no use now, I'm locked in; that parole officer isn't even likely to let me stay out on parole long.[27] His assessment was quite accurate.

25. The classic description of this is to be found in W. I. Thomas and F. Znaniecki, *The Polish Peasant in America and Poland* (New York: Knopf, 1918) where Polish girls are depicted as attracted by the shop "windows, theaters, the press, street life with its display of wealth, beauty and fashion, all (in) striking contrast to the monotony of the prospect which awaits her if she remains a 'good girl' . . . she feels that some small part . . . of the gorgeousness actually is within her reach, and her imagination pictures to her indefinite possibilities of further advance in the future." (Vol. II, pp. 1810-21.)

26. Clifford Shaw, *The Natural History of a Delinquent Career* (Chicago: University of Chicago Press, 1931).

27. From an interview done on a study directed by Eliot Studt at The Center for Law and Society, Universisy of California, Berkeley.

Temporal Articulation

In noting how variables such as direction, distance, and sign clarity affect temporal commitments to mobility and rates of mobility, we have already touched on another important issue: the temporal articulation of actions aimed toward mobility. Unless the phrasing and timing of those actions are properly managed, a person's mobility goals (whatever they are) are liable to go awry, even drastically.

Because mobility actions occur over time and are usually intermittent and meshed with many other kinds of acts, temporal articulation necessarily involves the careful management of transitional phases during the course of mobility. A monkey wrench can be thrown into phasing by circumstances outside the control of a person: a lengthy illness, or draft into the army, or being recalled to a failing family business may interrupt a promising occupational career and cause its abandonment. Circumstances within one's control can, however, also hinder or block mobility, as when a patriotic man enlists in the army at the beginning of a war, causing him to fall behind in the normal pursuit of his career;[28] or when a man chooses to have children but then must slow down or give up his professional career. Choices such as the foregoing immediately suggest the juggling of values and temporal commitments that are involved — sometimes silently and covertly — in maintaining courses of mobility in proper phase. The mismanagement of juggling becomes very apparent when a married couple does not yet want children, but unhappily the wife conceives; or when a man works so furiously that his neglected wife asks for a divorce.

Another potential source of misarticulation is the universal escalator on which everyone rides: the life cycle. Some mobility routes are rather closely linked with age grading so that inordinate departure from normal phasing can have serious consequences, either for the person himself or for his mobility. Children who become movie stars at tender ages, quite literally shooting sky high in income and prestige, face tremendous problems of personal adjustment as they grow older. They have "made it" far too early in the adult world. Musical prodigies have still another problem: they have been tremendously mobile,

28. "If he had not gone, had stayed put, there would have been no doubt about anything at the bank," Marquand, *op. cit.,* p. 125.

but as they become older can they stay on top? Not only do most not remain successful, many even leave the world of music. Of course, upwardly mobile persons can "arrive" too late in the life-cycle (too tired, sick, or psychologically worn out) really to enjoy their successes or, in a stylistic sense, to know what to do with the success. In mid-life, by changing occupational careers, some people move upward in status — nevertheless cannot move up as far as they might if they had started earlier or if old age did not foreclose on their movement so soon. Conversely, a demotion or a business disaster may arrive so late in life that an elderly man cannot recover totally and sometimes not at all.

For mobility routes whose phases are relatively scheduled, there are certain characteristic accompaniments, but if these go awry, mobility may be affected. There is "promised time" when junior executives are promised steady advance on a regular schedule (though the final stopping point may be left unspecified). However, if there is a betrayal of the promise or if company feuds break the requisite line of sponsorship, promised time turns out to be false time and mobility suffers. (Of course, there can be promised and false time for the downwardly mobile also.) There is also lead time, during which planning can go on for the scheduled next phase or phases. If the upward or downward mobility proceeds too quickly or if the person does not know about lead time, he can be at considerable disadvantage in coping with his phasing. Another accompaniment of scheduled phases is "time out" — time for respite, retreat, renewal, reviewal, even for play or expressive release of tension. In a genuine sense, this period may neither be time out nor time lost, but really the next phase along a mobility route. Frequently the year in Europe after or during college functions as a next or interim phase.

Although a man may be moving in accordance with conventional scheduling, there can be discernible consequences for him if others are moving faster or slower. After World War II and then again in recent years, men who had moved up the academic ladder at conventional rates were horrified and angry at the speed with which young men were promoted. Often the latter pulled even with the older men fairly quickly.[29] Some of the resulting sense of insult was reduced because

29. Just the opposite has happened with air pilots who in the early years of the

the disjuncture in rates was so widespread nationally and because nothing could be done about the situation because colleges and universities were in a competitive market. Yet there was, and still is, considerable tension in the academic air because of this situation. In business firms, favored men get promoted faster than others, with consequences for the latters' personal esteem and for their functioning within the organization. The situation is compounded when the fast mover is put in charge of slower movers, especially if they are older than he. When men are demoted or blocked, rather than promoted on schedule, this misphasing also, of course, has untoward personal and organizational consequences.

When phases are not clearly scheduled, or when there are differing expectations about those phases, other kinds of misarticulation consequences ensue, such as argumentation, accusations of negligence or betrayal, and other tension-laden interactions. A contemporary example is the disappointment, frustration and anger evinced by ghetto residents who expect jobs after their job corps training, but who then discover that there is no such next phase. When there is expectation of collective mobility, there is a possibility of great disagreement on proper phasing — witness the views of William Du Bois versus those of Booker T. Washington, or, nowadays, the impatience of blacks over their negligible upward mobility compared with the slower-paced expectations of whites about black mobility.

Analysis of phasing moves easily into consideration of timing (or pacing) as an aspect of articulation. If the chorus girl who wants to marry upward (in the classic tactical problem) plays the field she may wait too long for the richest man whom she might snare, and eventually — given her advancing years — she must settle for less than she might have gotten earlier. But if she marries too soon, she may not marry as wealthy a man as she might by waiting longer. The kinds of skills at pacing that some people develop are amusingly illustrated by Jerome Weidman's appropriately titled story, "I Knew What I Was Doing". The story line is about a woman who models dresses in a small manufacturing firm. She had piggybacked upward from dates with lower echelon personnel to higher status ones, until the manufac-

---

business took much less time to rise through the ranks than has been possible since the 1950s. *Cf.* Wesley Wagner, Ph. D. thesis, University of Chicago; also reported in Roth in B. Glaser, *op. cit.*

turer himself wanted to marry her — just as she was about to jump
from him to a big-time salesman who worked for a large company.
Her response was to think angrily:

> Who did he think he was anyway? What did I work myself up from heels
> like Jack and Weiss for? What did I work out the system for, getting it
> down to the point where it couldn't miss? So I should bury myself by
> marrying a dumb dress manufacturer and let the whole thing go to waste?
> . . .I knew just where I stood. As long as the world was full of guys like
> Robert Roberts, I wasn't stopping until I reached the top. What the hell
> did I want with a dope like Dave Cantor? "Forget it, Dave," I said. . .
> "You can keep it," I said, pushing the marriage license away from me. "
> Paste it in your hat," I said.[30]

Another kind of timing tactic is equally nicely illustrated by the song
of the chorus girl in *Guys and Dolls* who, tired of being a mistress for
so many years, quickly brings her man to marriage with her scornful
"Take Back Your Mink." Her tactic goes by various names, such as
"make up your mind" or the more vulgar "get on or off the pot, but
get going." American movie makers have elaborated *ad nauseum* on
this particular theme. The tactic, however, is general and often based
on considerations of awareness — catching the other when he is off his
guard.

   The subject of timing is so recognizable that there is danger of
belaboring it; but I shall run that risk by noting that timing is indis-
solubly linked with the structural situation in which the mobile person
and related others find themselves. Their tactics and counter tactics
cannot be understood except within pertinent structural contexts. As
one example, consider the career of the air pilot, as described in a
study by Wesley Wager.[31] The pilot is on an escalator, moving upward
inexorably to the top position of senior pilot. Below the top, if he fails
a crucial test at any point, he is not demoted but simply is "out." A
pilot can, however, speed up or slow down certain phases of his
upward climb. Within limits, he can put off going to upgrading
schools for a time, balancing his stalling of those phased assignments
against making a consequent bad impression on his superiors. A
co-pilot can hasten his upgrading by maneuvering for assignment with
captains who have reputations for allowing subordinates opportuni-

   30. Reprinted from *The Horse That Could Whistle Dixie,* in Seymour Krim (Ed.),
Manhattan (New York: Bantam Books, 1954), pp. 1-15.
   31. *Op. cit.*

ties to pilot the planes. He can choose a "home airport" where competition is lower than elsewhere because there are fewer senior pilots there, and so he is not yet prepared for promotion. To manage such a pacing, a pilot needs adequate information about the various assignments, airports, and senior pilots; but pilots are not very informed about such matters, especially the junior co-pilots who, perhaps, most need that information. An important but unplanned function of the upgrading schools "is to bring together groups of pilots at about the same career stage in one place for a number of weeks where they can informally exchange such relevant and important information.

The variable of awareness is of crucial importance in proper timing. The examples given earlier of men who either cannot or do not — though others warn them — correctly anticipate the last phases of their lives and consequently suffer downward mobility then or must work very hard not to lose income and position, are clear instances of this point. Just as clear are those instances — the reader can supply his own cases — where many a mobility opportunity (up or down) is missed because a man acted too slowly or quickly, because of inadequate information or simple ignorance or because of someone else's successful attempt to keep him blissfully uninformed and unaware.

Timing is not entirely a matter of skill, Machiavellian or otherwise. Either proper timing or unfortunate mistiming may rest entirely on fortuitous circumstance, as the typical turning point in Horatio Alger's famous stories reminds us. Of course, Alger never allowed his audiences to forget that aleatory circumstance — the blessed opportunity for the poor boy to stop the rich man's runaway horse — needed always to be followed up by the young hero's timely words and deed, as well as by proper future phasing of his relations with the appreciative benefactor.

9. GENERATING FORMAL THEORY

OUR APPROACH to the generation of grounded formal theory has been developed through some years of experience in doing research and in writing theory at varying levels of conceptualization. We have always tried to generate theory that fits the real world, works in predictions and explanations, is relevant to the people concerned, and that is readily modifiable.

Sources of Formal Theory

The several sources of formal theory can usefully be classified in three ways: grounded in systematic research, ungrounded, or a combination of both grounded and ungrounded. Speculative or ungrounded theory derives from any combination of several sources: whimsy and wisdoms of usually deceased great men, conjecture and assumptions about the "oughts" of life, and other extant speculative theory.[1] The

1. *Cf.* Peter Blau, *Exchange and Power in Social Life* (New York: John Wiley and Sons, 1964).

usual method of developing theory is to deduct logically from these sources. The weaving in of some grounded theory usually helps, but does not save nor even compete well with the theorist's emphasis on speculative sources.

As we have argued elsewhere,[2] this kind of formal theory does not meet our criteria of fit, "works," relevance, and easy modification. Indeed, because it is ungrounded, when applied to data such theory *forces* the data in many ways. The theory dictates, before empirical examination, presumed relevancies in problems, concepts, and hypotheses, and the kinds of the indicators that "should" apply — to the neglect of emergent relevancies of concepts, properties, and indicators. Its fit and its predictions also are suspect; while modification of the theory when it does not work is regarded as requiring systematic conclusive proof, certainly not warranted by a few exceptional (often crucial) incidents. This forcing of the theory has these consequences: some, especially young, theorists are dissuaded from advancing and extending theories, while other men settle for description made at low conceptual levels.

The principal sources of grounded theory consist both of the data of diverse systematic research and the substantive theories generated from such data. In combination and separately these sources give rise to three bases of grounding: (1) data, (2) substantive theory and (3) a combination of data and substantive theory. Combinations of data and theory are quite appropriate. The approach that one elects to use depends on the prior substantive research and theory development applicable to the formal area. Before considering each of the three bases of grounding and where our book is located with regard to them, let us briefly consider the essential difference and a few relationships between substantive and formal theory.

By *substantive theory* we mean that theory developed for a substantive or empirical area of sociological inquiry — such as patient care, race relations, professional education, geriatric life styles, delinquency, or financial organizations. By *formal theory* we mean that theory developed for a formal or conceptual area of sociological inquiry — such as status passage, stigma, deviant behavior, socialization, status congruency, authority and power, reward systems,

2. Barney G. Glaser and Anselm L. Strauss, *Discovery of Grounded Theory* (Chicago: Aldine Publishing Company, 1967).

organizations or organizational careers. Both types of theory may be considered "middle-range." They fall between the "minor working hypotheses" of everyday life and the "all-inclusive" grand theories.[3]

Substantive and formal theories exist on distinguishable levels of generality, which differ only in terms of degree. Therefore, in any one study each type of theory can shade at points into the other. The analyst, however, should focus clearly on one level or the other, or on a specific combination, because the strategies vary for arriving at each one. For example, in an analysis of the organizational careers of scientists, the focus was on the substantive area of scientists' careers, not on the formal area of organizational careers.[4] With the focus on such a substantive area, the generation of theory can be achieved by doing a comparative analysis between or among groups within the same substantive area. In this instance, comparisons were made among the career stages of junior investigator, senior investigator, and supervisor within two different promotional systems of the organization. Generation of the substantive theory also can be furthered by comparisons of the organizational careers of scientists with other substantive cases within the formal area of organizational careers, such as those of lawyers or military officers. Those comparisons would illuminate the substantive theory about scientists' careers.

However, if the focus of level of generality is on generating formal theory, the comparative analysis is made among different kinds of substantive cases and their theories, which fall within the formal area, without relating the resulting theory to any one particular substantive area. The focus of comparisons, to continue with our example, is now on generating a formal theory of organizational careers (in this case based on theories) not on generating a theory about a single substantive case of an organizational career.[5]

There are two principal ways that formal theory is generated from grounded substantive theory when no more data is involved. One is to advance the substantive to formal theory by a "rewriting technique,"[6] and the other is to analyze comparatively several diverse

3. See Robert K. Merton, *Social Theory and Social Structure* (New York: The Free Press, 1957), pp. 5-10.

4. Barney G. Glaser, *Organizational Scientists: Their Professional Careers* (Indianapolis, Bobbs-Merrill, 1964).

5. Barney G. Glaser (Ed.), *Organizational Careers: A Sourcebook for Theory* (Chicago: Aldine Publishing Company, 1968).

6. Glaser and Strauss, *Discovery*, pp. 8-92, 47-69.

substantive theories, as done in *Organizational Careers.* The latter is by far the more powerful of the two approaches: because of its coverage of more diverse properties of the theoretical area, it applies to more diverse substantive areas with minimal qualification. The former approach is, however, the more prevalent.

One version of rewriting techniques is simply to omit substantive words, phrases, or adjectives: instead of writing "temporal aspects of *dying* as a nonscheduled status passage," one would write "temporal aspects of nonscheduled status passage." Substantive theory can also be rewritten up a notch: instead of writing about how doctors and nurses give medical attention to a dying patient according to his social value, one would talk of how professional services are distributed according to the social value of clients.

In each version of the rewriting technique, the social scientist writes a one-area formal theory on the basis of his substantive theory: he does not generate the former directly from the data. These techniques produce only an adequate start toward formal theory, not an adequate formal theory itself. The researcher has raised the conceptual level of his work mechanically; he has not raised it through comparative understanding. He has done nothing to broaden the scope of his theory on the formal level by comparative investigation of different substantive areas. He has not escaped the time and place of his substantive research. Moreover, the formal theory cannot fit or work very well when written from only one substantive area (and often only one case of the area), because really it cannot be developed sufficiently to take into account all the contingencies and qualifications that will be met in the diverse substantive areas to which it will be applied. All that happens is that it will be modified by other theories and data through the comparative method, because by itself it is too sparsely developed to use in making trustworthy predictions and explanations. Thus the one-area formal theory remains, in actuality, treated as a substantive theory possibly later to be generalized by comparative analysis. To be sure such theory is a strategic link in advancing from substantive to formal theory, as is also the comparative analysis of several substantive theories.

This linkage between research data and formal theory, provided by substantive theory, also occurs when a particular substantive theory is extended and raised to formal theory by the comparative analysis of other data.[7] The linkage occurs also when the substantive theory is comparatively analyzed both with other substantive theories and with research data, as in this book on status passage. This linkage is not omitted when generating a formal theory from diverse sets of data. It is natural to the process of generating that parts of a substantive theory will emerge from the initial set of substantive data, before the theory's level of conceptualization is raised by comparing it to data drawn from other substantive areas.

Substantive theories typically have important general relevance and become, almost automatically, springboards or stepping stones to the development of a grounded formal theory. For example, a substantive theory on the comparative failure of scientists[8] leads directly to the need for a theory of comparative failure in work (or even more generally in all facets of social life). Or substantive theory on deviance disavowal of people with visible handicaps leads to one concerned with deviance disavowal by a much wider range of persons.[9]

Other aspects of the link between research data and grounded formal theory, provided by substantive theory, are the providing of initial direction in developing relevant conceptual categories, conceptual properties of categories, hypotheses relating these concepts, and in choosing possible modes of integration for the theory. We emphasize "initial" because — as the formal theory is generated from comparing many substantive theoretical ideas from many different cases — the relevant categories, properties, and hypotheses can change in the process of generating theory. Also, in integrating formal theory, formal models of process, structure, and analysis may be useful guides to integration, along with models provided by the comparatively analyzed substantive theories. Our approach to grounding theory underlines the point that the formal theory we are talking about is induced by comparative analysis and must be contrasted with "grand" theory that is generated by logical deduction from assumptions and speculations about the "oughts" of social life.

7. This method is exemplified in Anselm Strauss' article *Discovering New Theory From Previous Theory*, in T. Shibutani (Ed.), Human Nature and Collective Behavior: Papers in Honor of Herbert Blumer (Englewood Cliffs, N. J. Prentice-Hall, 1970).

8. Barney G. Glaser, "Comparative Failure of Scientists," in *Science,* March 6, 1964, Vol. 143, pp. 1012-14.

9. Fred Davis, "Deviance Disavowal," *Social Problems,* IX (1961) pp. 120-132.

Within these relations between social research, substantive theory and formal theory is a design for the cumulative nature of knowledge and theory. The design involves a progressive building up from facts through substantive to formal grounded theory. To generate grounded substantive theory we need many facts for the necessary comparative analysis; ethnographic studies and direct data collection are required. Ethnographic studies, substantive theories, and direct data collection are all, in turn, necessary for building up by comparative analysis to formal theory. This design, then, locates the place of each level of work within the cumulation of knowledge and theory, and thereby suggests a divison of labor in sociological work.

For example, having developed this theory of status passage there is no reason not to link other *grounded* theory with ours, providing this extant theory fits well and makes sense of our data. In the foregoing chapters, "awareness theory" was linked with our emergent theory of status passage. Useful linkages with other grounded theories possibly will occur to other readers. In turn, our theory of status passage is subject to extension by colleagues — best done through theoretical sampling and the associated comparative analysis. This extension represents a further specifying of the limits of our theory and thus an inevitable qualification of it.

If we do not practice such modes of extending grounded theories, we relegate them, particularly if substantive, mainly to the status of respected little islands of knowledge, separated from others — each visited from time to time by inveterate footnoters, by assemblers of readings and of periodic bibliographical reviews, and by graduate students assigned to read the better literature. While the owners of these islands understandably are pleased to be visited, in due course of time they can look forward to falling out of fashion and to being bypassed. This is no way to build a cumulative body of theory.

We may even discover eventually that one bit of theory never really was theory, a discovery made about Merton's famous anomie paper. As the Merton example illustrates, another consequence of failing to delimit, extend, and diversify extant grounded theory is that sociologists continue to develop both speculative theory and general theoretical frameworks without recognizing the great difference between those formulations and theory that is genuinely grounded in data. However useful the former types may be as rhetoric or for orientation, taken as theory they simply help to forestall another generation's discovery and formulation of testable theory. Speculative theory and theoretical frameworks also have had the consequence of turning away many from theorizing (because those are the only theories they recognize) in favor of syntheses[10] or publishing low-level description. The description is a necessary sociological task but comparable to zoologists' collecting of specimens and making of primitive classification — a far cry from creating effective theory.

The cumulative design also suggests that, besides ethnographic studies, *multiple* substantive and formal theories are needed to build up, through discovering their relationships, to more inclusive formal theories. Such a call for multiple theories is in contrast to the directly monopolistic implication of logico-deductive theories, whose formulators talk as if there is only one theory for a formal area or perhaps only one formal sociological theory for all areas. The need for multiple substantive theories to generate a formal theory may be obvious, but it is not so obvious that multiple formal theories are also necessary. One formal theory never handles all the relevancies of an area, and by comparing many formal theories we can begin to arrive at more inclusive, parsimonious levels of formal theory. Parsimonious grounded formal theories are hard won by this design. The logico-deductive theorist, proceeding under the license and mandate of analytic abstraction and deduction from assumptions and conjecture, engages in premature parsimony of form. He is not concerned with the theoretical comparative analysis of data and substantive theories required to achieve a theory that fits and works in explaining and interpreting a formal area of inquiry.

Generating Formal Theory by Comparative Analysis

The term *comparative analysis* — often used in sociology and anthropology — has grown to encompass several different meanings and thereby to carry several different burdens. Many sociologists and anthropologists, recognizing the great power of comparative analysis, have employed it for achieving their various purposes. To avoid confusion we must, therefore, be clear as to our own use for comparative

10. John Lofland, *Deviance and Identity* (Englewood Cliffs, New Jersey, Prentice-Hall, 1969).

analysis (generating of theory) in contrast to its other uses (achieving accurate evidence, empirical generalizations, specification of a concept, and verifications of a hypothesis). Generation of theory both subsumes and assumes these other uses, but only to the extent that they are in the service of generation. Otherwise they are sure to stifle it.

Comparative analysis is considered a general method, in our use of it, just as are the experimental and statistical methods — all involve the logic of comparisons. Comparative analysis can, like those other methods, be used for social units of any size. Some sociologists and anthropologists customarily use the term "comparative analysis" to refer only to comparisons among large scale social units, particularly organizations, nations, institutions, and large regions of the world. But such a reference restricts a general method to use with only the specific class of social units to which it has frequently been applied. As a general method for generating theory, comparative analysis takes on its fullest generality when one realizes its power applied to social units of any size, large or small, ranging from men or their roles to the nations or world regions. It can also be used to compare conceptual units of a theory or theories, as well as data, such as categories and their properties and hypotheses. This results in generating, densifying, and integrating the theories into a formal theory by discovering a more parsimonious set of concepts with greater scope.

The basic criterion governing the selection of comparison groups for generating theory is their *theoretical relevance* for furthering the development of emerging categories, properties, hypotheses, and integration of the theory. Any groups may be selected that will help generate these elements of the theory.

In making his selections, the researcher must always remember that he is an active sampler of theoretically relevant data, not an ethnographer trying to get the fullest data on a group with or without a preplanned research design. As an active sampler of data, he must continually analyze the data to see where the next theoretical question will take him.

In theoretical sampling, no one kind of data on a category nor any single technique for data collection is necessarily appropriate. Different kinds of data give the analyst different views or vantage points from which to understand a category and to develop its proper-

ties; these different views we have called "slices of data". Theoretical
sampling allows a multi-faceted investigation: there are no limits to
the techniques of data collection, the way they are used, or the types
of data required. The result is a variety of slices of data that would
be bewildering if one wishes to evaluate them as accurate evidence for
verifications. However, for generating theory this variety is highly
beneficial, because it yields more information on categories than any
one mode of knowing (technique of collection). Among the slices of
data that can be used is the "anecdotal comparison." Through his own
experiences, general knowledge or reading, and the stories of others,
the social scientist can gain data on other groups that offer useful
comparisons. Anecdotal comparisons are especially useful in developing core categories. The researcher can ask himself where else has he
learned about the category, and make quick comparisons to start to
develop it and sensitize himself to its relevancies.

Rules of comparability of groups used in descriptive and verification studies do not apply in generating theory because *group comparisons* are conceptual. Conceptual comparisons are made by comparing
diverse or similar evidence from different groups which indicate the
same conceptual categories and properties, not by comparing the
evidence for its own sake. Or, they are made by comparing theoretical
concepts grounded in each group, or by comparing evidence for a
concept from one group to a concept already developed from another.
Comparative analysis of concepts or their indicators takes full advantage of the "interchangeability" of indicators and develops, as it proceeds, a broad range of acceptable indicators for categories and
properties.

Two typical rules of comparability are especially *irrelevant* when
generating theory is the goal. One rule states that to be included
within a set of comparison groups a group must have enough features
in common with them. Another rule is that to be excluded it must
show a "fundamental difference" from the others. These two rules for
verificational and descriptive studies attempt to hold constant the
strategic facts or to disqualify groups where the facts either cannot
actually be constant or would introduce more unwanted differences.
In sum, one hopes that in this set of purified comparison groups
spurious factors will not influence the findings and relationships and
render them inaccurate.

These rules hinder the generation of theory. Weeding out spurious factors is not important in generating since they are just one more theoretical idea to be included in the theory. Indeed, concern with these rules — to avoid spuriousness and inaccuracy — diverts attention away from the important sets of fundamental differences and similarities among groups which, upon analysis, become important qualifying conditions under which categories and properties vary. These conditions should be made a vital part of the theory. Further, these two rules hinder the use of a wider range of groups for developing categories and properties. Such a range, necessary for the categories' fullest possible development, is achieved by comparing *any* group, irrespective of differences or similarities, as long as the data indicate a similar category or property.

When theoretically sampling for comparison groups, several matters must be kept in mind. The analyst must be clear on the basic *types* of groups he wishes to compare in order to control their effect on the generality of both *scope* of population and *conceptual level* of his theory. The simplest comparisons are made among different groups of exactly the same substantive type; for instance, different federal bookkeeping departments. These comparisons lead to a substantive theory that is applicable to this one type of group. Somewhat more general substantive theory is achieved by comparing different types of groups; for example, different kinds of federal departments in one federal agency. The scope of the theory is further increased by comparing different types of groups within different larger groups (different departments in different agencies). Generality is further increased by making these latter comparisons for different regions of a nation, or, to go further, different nations. *The scope of a substantive theory can be carefully increased and controlled by such conscious choices of groups.* For substantive theory, one can select groups within the same substantive class regardless of where he finds them. He can, thus, compare the "emergency ward" to all kinds of medical wards in all kinds of hospitals both in the United States and abroad. But he may also conceive of the emergency ward as a subclass of a larger class of organizations, all designed to render immediate assistance in the event of accidents or breakdowns of any kind. For example, fire, crime, riots, the automobile, and even plumbing problems have all given rise to emergency organizations that are on twenty-four hour alert. In taking this approach to choosing dissimilar, substantive comparative groups, the analyst must be clear about his purpose. He may use groups of the more general class to illuminate his substantive theory of, say, emergency wards. He may wish to begin generating a formal theory of emergency organizations. He may desire a mixture of both: for instance, bring out his substantive theory about emergency wards within a context of some formal categories about emergency organizations.

When the aim is to discover formal theory, as was ours, the analyst will definitely select dissimilar substantive groups from the larger class, in order to increase his theory's scope while transcending substantive areas. He will also find himself comparing groups that seem to be non-comparable on the substantive level but which on the formal level are conceptually comparable. Noncomparable on the substantive level here implies a stronger degree of apparent difference than does dissimilar. For example, while fire departments and emergency wards are substantially dissimilar, the conceptual comparability is still readily apparent.

Since the basis of comparison between substantively non-comparable groups is not readily apparent, it must be explained on a higher conceptual level. For example, one could start developing a formal theory of social isolation by comparing four apparently unconnected monographs: *Blue Collar Marriage, The Taxi-Dance Hall, The Ghetto,* and *The Hobo.*[11] All deal with facets of "social isolation," according to their authors. For another example, Goffman has compared apparently non-comparable groups when generating his formal theory of stigma.[12] Anyone who wishes to discover formal theory, then, should be aware of the usefulness of comparisons made on high level conceptual categories among the seemingly noncomparable. He should actively seek this kind of comparison, do it with flexibility, and be able to interchange the apparently non-comparable comparison with the apparently comparable ones. The non-comparable type of group comparison can greatly aid him in transcending substantive

11. Mirra Komarovsky, *Blue Collar Marriage* (New York: Random House, 1962); Paul Cressey, *The Taxi-Dance Hall* (Chicago: University of Chicago Press, 1932); Louis Wirth, *The Ghetto* (Chicago: University of Chicago Press, 1962 edition); and Nels Anderson, *The Hobo* (Chicago: University of Chicago Press, 1961 edition).
12. Erving Goffman, *Stigma* (Englewood Cliffs: Prentice-Hall, 1963).

descriptions of time and place as he tries to generate a general, formal theory.

Our Selection of Comparisons

The method of comparative analysis used to generate a formal theory of status passage has dictated the theoretical criteria for choosing data and theory for this volume. The current state of sociological and anthropological study of status passage is that there are some substantive theories on similar and diverse aspects and problems of, and much research data on, status passage. The next step was to put them together for a comparative analysis that would generate formal theory on aspects of status passage.

The principal criterion for selecting our materials was *ideational* — to provide as broad and diverse a range of theoretical ideas on status passage as possible. *This range of ideas may be contrasted to, and does not necessarily mean, a broad range of data or of authors.* Thus, the materials have been chosen to provide as many categories, properties, hypotheses, and problems on status passage as space permitted — which, in turn, provided the elements for developing the formal theory.

Most of our materials came from exploratory qualitative research, (and not all are published) for in this form of research we usually find an abundance of general categories, hypotheses, and problems, in contrast to their sparseness in quantitative research. Since the data on status passage is abundant, while writings with substantive theoretical ideas grounded in data are far fewer, the utilized range of authors and data is, obviously, not as great as it could be — but it need not be that great. Further, the data or grounded theory from one author's work can be used in several places in our theory, since ideas that fit theoretical areas or problems are the criterion of placement — *not* how much of an author or of a kind of data is used.

It will be readily apparent indeed that the ideas of many of the materials are applicable to several parts of the book. But each is put where it will contribute the most ideationally to the generation of our theory. The reader may, however, read sections or chapters with another perspective more suitable to whatever he is currently studying. For example, he may study the chapters on reversibility and temporality to help his study of "promotion."

Because our groups may be chosen for a single comparison only, we had no definite, prescribed, preplanned set to compare for all or even most categories (as there are in comparative studies made for accurate descriptions and verification). In research carried out for discovering theory, the researcher cannot cite the number and types of groups from which he collected data until the research is completed. In an extreme case, he may then find that the development of each major category may have been based on comparisons of different sets of groups. In our case there was considerable overlap of comparison groups.

Theoretical Formulation

It is important to note that the formulation of grounded theory may take different forms. Although we consider the *process* of generating theory as inextricably related to its subsequent use and effectiveness in research and application, the *form* in which the theory is presented can be (but is best not) independent of this process by which it was generated. Grounded theory, whether formal or substantive, can be presented either as a well codified or axiomatically developed set of propositions as well as in a running theoretical discussion, using conceptual categories and their properties as elements in the hypotheses, which are the generalized relations between them.

We have chosen the discussional form for several reasons.[13] Our strategy of comparative analysis for generating theory puts a high emphasis on *theory as process;* that is, theory as an ever-developing entity, to be extended and modified, not as a perfected product merely to be negated. The discussional form renders this emphasis better, and renders better also its relation to the grounding process by which it is generated. To be sure, theory as process eventually must be presented in publications as a product, but it is written with the assump-

13. This choice is not new, because most theory is written this way, whether grounded or logico-deductive. But we have noted this decision, on the request of several colleagues, to fend off the critique that the only true theory is the one written, by the numbers, as an integrated set of propositions. The form in which a theory is presented does not make it a theory; it is a theory because it explains or predicts something.

tion that it is a product only for the moment and is still developing. Theory as process, we believe, renders quite well the reality of social interaction and its structural context. The discussional form of formulating theory gives a feeling of "ever-developing" and "modifiability" to the theory, allows it to become quite rich in complexity, integration and density and makes its fit and relevance to reality easy to comprehend.

In contrast, to state a theory in propositional form would make it less complex, dense, and rich and more laborious to read. It would also tend by implication to "freeze" the theory instead of giving the feeling of a need for continued development. When necessary for a verificational study, parts of a theoretical discussion can at any point be rephrased as a set of propositions. This rephrasing is simply a formal exercise — usually required of students — since the concepts are already related in the discussion.

Also, with either a propositional or discussional grounded theory, the sociologist then can logically deduce further hypotheses. Deduction from grounded theory, as it develops, is the method by which the researcher directs his theoretical sampling for more comparative groups.

Making a distinction between category and property indicates a systematic relationship between these two elements of theory. A category stands by itself as a conceptual element of theory; for example, a reversal. A property, in turn, is a conceptual aspect or element of a category; for example, the degree of clarity of a reversal. Both are concepts indicated by the data (and are not the data itself). Once a category or property is conceived, change in the evidence that indicated it will not destroy it. The change in data — more and different indicators are discovered — may only modify or clarify it, if any effect is warranted. Conceptual categories and properties have a life apart from the evidence that gave rise to them, as for example, they are seen to fit and to be relevant to data in vastly different social realms. For example, sentimental recapitulation — a concept generated from research on college class reunions — also applies to aspects of lawsuits and charter groups of new organizations.

Categories and properties vary in degree of conceptual abstraction. Synthesis and integration of the theory may occur at many levels of conceptual and hypothetical generalization, whether varying from substantive to formal theory or within the formal level of abstraction. Levels of conceptualization, then, is one aspect of the *density* of generated grounded theory. Another aspect of density is how densely a category is developed in terms of its theoretical properties; yet another consideration is how well the theory is integrated within its full range of conceptualization. *We believe that a generated theory warrants much densification* so that it will fit a multitude of situations in the area it is purported to explain. A dense theory lends itself to ready modification and formulation in order to handle yet new qualifications required by changing conditions in what is "going on." A dense theory helps relate very abstract levels to data.

Several kinds of theoretical ideas are useful in generating the dense, property development of a category. The analyst is literally forced by comparative analysis to think in terms of the full range or types, degree, or continua of a category, its dimensions, the conditions and contingencies under which it exists or is pronounced or minimized, its major consequences, its structural context, the social and structural processes that bring it about or maintain it, the strategies people use to control or handle it, its relationship to other categories and their properties. Examples of these ideas are found woven into the theory offered in this volume.

The integration of a dense formal theory is accomplished quite differently than that of a substantive theory. The latter is integrated by the emergence of a natural integration which occurs in the data of the area under consideration. Not so for formal theory: integration of small segments of a formal theory do emerge as it is generated, as seen in the sections of this book, but in large measure the total integration of the formal theory is arbitrary. Hence, the theory must be integrated by one or more theoretical models. In our case, we chose a cumulative build-up of several core categories of status passage, each of which has clear relationships to the other. Thus, direction and timing combine to make shape; and desirability provides the motivation to control shape and to go through a single status passage, through multiple status passages and alone, in aggregate and in concert.

This mode of integrating the theory readily can be seen as arbitrary, in light of possible alternative modes. We originally worked on fifteen core categories of status-passage,[14] which could have been reduced differently than as we finally chose; and of course we did not work on all possible core categories.

Our integrative model had three clear consequences for the theory. First, how the ideas were sorted out and assigned among chapters may appear arbitrary. For example, the reader easily may see where ideas on reversibility could have been put into the chapter on shape. Second, readers quickly should see gaps and new directions for our theory. Since it is impossible to saturate when generating formal theory (although saturation is probable in generating substantive theory), our claim is only to have developed what we were interested in and considered relevant in its own right — being mindful that other categories not touched on may be equally interesting and relevant. These constitute other areas that other theorists may fruitfully work on; for example the circumstantiality and the centrality of status passages need much more study. Third, our theory when submitted to further thought and brought into conjunction with more comparative data can easily be modified and extended. It will thereby gain in scope. Given these three consequences, our model and approach are only a beginning for those colleagues who wish to go beyond our treatment of status passages. For those who wish to use the theory in their own research, however, its coverage even now is quite extensive.

One clear consequence of both high density and tight integration of ideas — in favor of a plethora of examples — is the relatively *unrelieved* nature of our book on status passages: it goes slow for the attentive reader. We can only advise readers to read quickly for the main ideas and for their integration into the theory; then to read at a slower pace in order to study their densification. Giving more examples would simply result in fewer ideas and scope: this would undermine the basic power of the theory. Indeed, we have only presented about one third of what we had generated for reasons of space and sanity. These remarks on the finiteness of space, and of our abilities and skills, relative to what possibility ideally could be accomplished leads next to the question: *how as people did we actually write this book?*

14. For some, see Anselm L. Strauss, "Some Neglected Properties of Status Passage", in Howard S. Becker *et al.* (Ed.), *Institutions and the Person* (Chicago: Aldine Publishing Company, 1968) pp. 265-71. These are also noted briefly in Chapter 1.

A Natural History of Our Theory

It is relevant first to know how our interest in status passages germinated. Both authors had considerable experience with notions about status passage before generating the theory developed in this book. Strauss came from the University of Chicago where ideas about careers — a popular form of research and theory on status passages — were being evolved by Everett Hughes and his students. With Howard S. Becker, Strauss analyzed comparatively these ideas, writing general theory in an article titled "Careers, Personality and Adult Socialization."[15] He started developing notions about status-passage in his *Mirrors and Masks.*[16] Further research on scientists, on medical education, nursing education and psychiatric hospitals dealt with aspects of careers or status passage.

Glaser studied at Columbia University and there was well steeped in status and role theory of the static variety, as then used in eastern sociology, but was quite ready to put status into motion. After meeting Strauss in 1960, he readily rewrote and published his dissertation as a study of the organizational careers of scientists. A few years later he published a reader on organizational careers,[17] attempting to develop formal theory for this particular type of status passage.

When we began studying dying patients in hospitals, we realized quickly that again we were dealing with several careers. The patient's illness and hospital careers were paramount. It was clear that another kind of status passage was being studied, so we decided that eventually, given the several careers we had studied, to analyze them and others comparatively to generate a theory of status passage. This book was the outcome of that decision.

Because so much relevant data and theory was "in" us from our previous work, the principal mode used to generate theory was to talk out our comparisons in lengthy conversations, and either record the conversation or take notes. We talked through virtually everything we could remember, and studied relevant literature for more data and

15. "Careers, Personality and Adult Socialization," *American Journal of Sociology,* 62 (Nov. 1956) pp. 253-63.
16. *Mirrors and Masks* (San Francisco: The Sociology Press, 1970).
17. *Op. cit.*

theory. These conversations went on almost five days a week for three months. At this time we gave up in exhaustion, and with the realization that we could begin to write it all up. We achieved writing about one third of our material, as mentioned earlier.

The benefits of collaboration were several. Between the two of us, we could cover a larger array of materials. We could also keep each other on the correct conceptual level, a task which is very difficult for the solo formal theorist who can easily get bogged in detail. Also the generating proceeds more quickly since each analyst takes off on the other's comments; then this reciprocally stimulates the former.

Frequently it was difficult to remember exactly what our previous conversation was about, so we trusted to maintaining continuity of discussion through ongoing reminders of what we had done before — while we proceeded each day by starting the conversation just about "anywhere." Thus we kept up each other's confidence that our analysis would, indeed, be extensive enough over time — without preconception — to arrive eventually at a theory of considerable scope. At some points xeroxing our notes and studying them helped to maintain continuity and coverage. Without such efforts, it would be easy constantly to inter-relate the same old ideas based on the same old assumptions — a typical condition of formal theorists.

These benefits of collaboration came speedily because they were based on previous writing of other books and articles together and on collaborating with other researchers. This preparation was invaluable because collaborating on the generation of formal theory is or at least seems more difficult than collaborating on substantive theory. Our lengthy preparation by no means implies that others cannot collaborate on formal theory from the start. They can profit from the method and strategies exemplified by and in our work. We would hope that they add to these methods when generating their formal theories.

After Formal Theory What?

Our colleagues often ask: what is there after formal theory? We assume that they accept the standard uses of formal theory: guiding substantive research; opening up areas for thought, research, and scholarship; verifying segments of it; modifying and extending it and integrating it with other theory to increase its scope with parsimony.

Other uses for grounded formal theory exist. These are based on the fact that it is not generalized to other populations cogently but can be *generalized to basic social processes that underlie the issues and problems of diverse substantive areas — for which there is yet no grounded theory.* This general relevance, this transcending of substantive areas, makes grounded formal theory a viable, applicable tool in, for example, consultations and during negotiations.

When using grounded formal theory, the social scientists need not know all there is to be known about the substantive area. A little substantive knowledge, related to the emergent fit of principal indicators, allows the formal theory to be applied. For example, theory about emergency systems that is based on the standard systems of a city, can be applied to developing a new system, such as a type of "crisis intervention." The consultant finds that the mind-absorbing and mind-opening aspects of such formal theory make sense to the client, and soon he becomes able to supply his own indicators and substantive information. Moreover, a theorist *qua* consultant can contribute to the research enterprises of colleagues, by stimulating thought about the implications of their data (already or soon to be collected) concerning matters suggested by grounded formal theory. We have found the theory of status passages useful both for research consultation and pragmatically addressed consultation.[18]

Often in the latter kind of consultation there is neither time nor money for the research needed to develop a relevant substantive theory; or there is yet nothing to research, or no way to research the data. Cogent suggestions are needed, and grounded formal theory is most applicable in these instances. Our theory of status passage, for instance, is fairly obviously applicable to help, guide, and articulate many institutionalized status passages now in their formation, expansion, or "having problems:" such as new kinds of training programs, illness careers, and novel styles of socialization.

18. After having developed the beginning outlines of another formal theory — about negotiation — we are convinced that particular theory can be useful, even in its primitive state, for helping resolve some problems encountered in various types of negotiations. The theory offers useful leads for arriving at just resolutions and compromises when negotiations are stalled or participants are obdurate. The theory can also be useful for stimulating work on negotiative aspects of substantive areas.

We have underlined the applied capability of grounded formal theory as an emerging area for sociological endeavor and theory.[19] Applied social theory — in contrast to applied social research — only becomes realistic with the development of grounded theory that fits, works, is relevant, and is readily modifiable.

19. Hans L. Zetterberg, *Social Theory and Social Practice* (Totowa, New Jersey: The Bedminister Press, 1962).

Index

distance in, 24
face-saving, 30
presence of alternative options,
  25
probability of and severity of, 25
relative import of, 26
See also False reversals;
  Re-reversal pattern
Reversibility, 4, 17–30
  personal conditions in
    affecting structural
      conditions, 27
    causing agent to make
      phasing difficult or easy, 28
    intensifying rigors at end of
      a leavable passage, 28
    as limitations of
      agent/passagee strategy, 27
    passagee's identity bound up
      in passage, 29
    passagee's misconceptions of
      self or passage, 30
  preventable, 17
    of a desirable passage, 17
    education as a mechanism
      of, 18
    of an undesirable passage, 17
  structural sources of, 21, 22
    change in passage direction
      by structure, 23
    emergence of new,
      higher-priority passage, 22
    lack of constant movement
      forward, 21
    structural generation of a
      crucial incident, 23
  See also Misconceptions
Rewrite technique, 178–179
Roth, J., 6, 10

Sanctions used by control agent, 72
Scapegoats, 121
Schulberg, B., 158
Scope of theory, 185
Sentimental order
  defined, 43
  disrupting effect of temporal
    changes, 43
  role of closed awareness context,
    43

in support of open awareness
  context, 45, 53
and unscheduled passages, 44
See also Temporal articulation
Sentimental journey. *See*
  Recapitulations
Shape of a passage
  definition of, 32, 57
  desired collective shape, deviance
    from, 125
  deviance from, resulting from
    failure to read signs of passage,
    73
  external sources of control in, 82,
    83
  knowledge of passage as control
    over, 68, 83, 84
  See also End-runner;
    Out of shape passages
Smigel, E. O., 61
Socially alienated passages, 92–94
Social mobility in America, temporal
  aspects of, 157–175
  quick social rise, favored over
    slow, delayed rise, 170
  slow social rises and descents,
    167
  swift social ascents and descents,
    167–170
  See also Groups without social
    mobility; Life-style; Rate of
    passage
Solo agent, aggregate passagees, 135–
  140
  agent maintenance of closed
    awareness context, 136
  agent view vs. passagee view, 135
  bargaining position of passagee,
    138
  competing demands of clients,
    136–137
  mutual voluntariness in, 137
  passagee leverage, 137
  silent control by passagee, 138–
    139
  taking competitors into
    advantageous account, 137
  use of consultants, 139
Solo passages, 4, 116, 140–141
  within collective passages, 123–
    124

Lightning Source UK Ltd.
Milton Keynes UK
UKOW05f0646130214

226389UK00002B/68/P